A MESSIANIC PERSPECTIVE ON THE

What About The Sacrifices?

D. THOMAS LANCASTER

A MESSIANIC PERSPECTIVE ON THE LEVITICAL PRIESTHOOD AND SACRIFICES

What About The Sacrifices?

D. THOMAS LANCASTER

FIRST FRUITS OF
ZION

First Edition 2011
Printed in the United States of America

ISBN: 978-1-892124-53-1

Cover Design: Joel Powell

Quantity discounts are available on bulk purchases of this book for educa-
tional, fundraising, or event purposes. Special versions or book excerpts to
fit specific needs are available from First Fruits of Zion. For more informa-
tion, contact www.ffoz.org/contact.

First Fruits of Zion

PO Box 649, Marshfield, Missouri 65706–0649 USA
Phone (417) 468–2741, www.ffoz.org

Comments and questions: www.ffoz.org/contact

Contents

Introduction
Why Study the Sacrifices?

> Why do we start the children with Leviticus and not with Genesis? The Holy One, Blessed be he, said, "Since the children are pure and the sacrifices are pure, let the pure come and occupy themselves with things that are pure." (*Leviticus Rabbah* 7:3)

When our Master Yeshua was five years old, he began to study the book of *Vayikra* (Leviticus). In the days of the Master (and even in modern Judaism) the formal religious education of a child begins at the age of five and with the study of this book. Leviticus may seem like an unnatural place to begin. The creation narratives, the story of the flood, or the call of Abraham might seem like a better place for a child to begin. Nonetheless, throughout Jewish history, children began their Bible studies in the book of Leviticus.

Why should little children be forced to study the dreadful laws of blood and sacrifice which constitute the first chapters of Leviticus? We would not impose a serious study of Leviticus even on our seminary students, much less our five-year-olds.

Our aversion to Leviticus is largely based upon our revulsion at the thought of animal sacrifice. The mainstream of western Christianity possesses an unconscious reluctance to acknowledge that our God is a God who not only chose to be worshipped through the sacrifice of animals but, in fact, took pleasure in the fragrance of burning meat rising from the altar. We have so sanitized and whitewashed God that the demand for animal sacrifice seems to contradict everything we believe about him. The laws of sacrifice, and sacrificing itself, disconcerts us. When the biblical text begins to teach us about priests throwing blood around and cutting out the fat surrounding the diaphragm and the two kidneys, we tend to become nauseous rather than blessed. We quickly explain that God only intended the sacrifices to teach the Israelites about the need for the Messiah's atonement, and we comfort ourselves with the notion that the New Testament abolishes sacrifice.

But this statement makes a gross oversimplification. The first several chapters of Leviticus present five different classifications of sacrifice, each brought for different reasons. The Bible speaks of dozens of different bread offerings, wine libations, other offerings, and of complex ritual procedures, and it has chapters and chapters of text describing sacrificial ceremonies, procedures for ordaining priests, and instructions for their sanctification and purification. The Torah is never stingy on details concerning the ritual services.

Of what value is it for us to profess that the Messiah fulfills the sacrifices when we know virtually nothing about those same sacrifices? To simply dismiss it all by saying, "Yeshua fulfilled the sacrifices," does a great disservice to the text and to the Master himself. If we truly believe that Yeshua's death and resurrection fulfilled the institutions of sacrifice and sacrificing, then we as believers are all the more obligated to invest our energy in studying those institutions, for only to the extent that we understand them can we hope to understand the work of Messiah.

In this booklet, we will spend some time thinking about the biblical sacrifices and the Levitical sacrificial system. I originally developed the material in this booklet for First Fruits of Zion's Torah Club programs, and the reader who wants to study the sacrificial system in greater detail can do so through the Torah Club commentaries. The selection of material comprising this booklet originally came together as First Fruits of Zion's audio study, "What About the Sacrifices?"

As we begin to study the laws of sacrifice, we need to keep in mind that, regardless of our own personal predilections, the sacrificial service is the method of worship which God ordained. Sacrifice is a universal religious reflex; human beings seem hardwired to recognize their need for atonement in the face of the divine. Consider the story of Cain and Abel sacrificing at the outset of humanity. Consider, too, that sacrifice in one form or another was universal in the world's ancient religions. The Torah puts form, structure, and definition around that God-given impulse.

Whether or not we approve of the rituals or think that they are rational is irrelevant; God has ordained them. Therefore we should be less concerned about why sacrifice was (or is) necessary and more concerned with what God intends to communicate to us by our obedience to his commandments.

Of course, without a Tabernacle or Temple, the laws of sacrifice seem largely irrelevant. It is not practical for us to keep any of these commandments in our time. To make a sacrifice today would, in itself, violate the laws of God's Torah.

Nevertheless, the study of the sacrifices from a Messianic perspective reconciles apparent discrepancies between the scriptures, corrects some common theological errors, illuminates the content of the book of Hebrews, and brings glory to our Master, who laid down his life as a living sacrifice on our behalf.

> Rabbi Yitzchak said, "What is the significance of the verses [in Leviticus] that say, 'This is the law of the sin offering,' and 'This is the law of the guilt offering?' They teach that any man who occupies himself with the study of the laws of the sin offering is regarded as if he was offering a sin offering, and any man who occupies himself with the study of the laws of the guilt offering is regarded as though he was offering a guilt offering." (b.*Menachot* 110a)

May the LORD bless every disciple who applies himself to learn about the holy sacrifices, the priesthood, the Temple, and their relationship to his Son.

D. THOMAS LANCASTER

Summary

The biblical education of Jewish children begins with Leviticus, a book largely about the sacrificial system. The animal sacrifices, however, are especially repugnant to modern Christians who see them as a temporary provision until Messiah's final atonement for sin. The Torah prescribes a variety of sacrifices, and less than half of these are for sin. Since Yeshua did not abrogate the Torah, neither did he cancel the sacrifices and offerings. By studying the sacrifices we gain insight into God's instructions for approaching him in worship, and a better understanding of Yeshua's work on our behalf.

Questions

1. Why do Jewish children begin their study of the Bible with Leviticus?
2. What is it about animal sacrifices that disturbs western Christians?
3. Besides animals, what are some other biblical sacrifices?
4. Why do Jews not offer sacrifices today?
5. Discuss: It is an oversimplification to say that Yeshua fulfills the sacrifices.

1

What Are the Sacrifices?

> So Moses finished the work. Then the cloud covered the tent of meeting, and the glory of the LORD filled the tabernacle. And Moses was not able to enter the tent of meeting because the cloud settled on it, and the glory of the LORD filled the tabernacle. (Exodus 40:33–35)

In the last chapter of Exodus, Moses and Israel encountered a problem with the new Tabernacle. It seemed that the Tabernacle was a success; the presence of God had taken up residence within it, and it served its function as the dwelling place of the Divine Presence. Yet a flaw with the concept immediately surfaced. Even if God could dwell among the Israelites in a holy place, that did not mean that the Israelites could have any communion or interaction with him. God was still holy; man was still unholy. How could the unholy man come near to the holy God? God was still transcendent, and man was not.

Moses faced this problem at the end of the book of Exodus. God had taken up residence in the Tabernacle, but he was unapproachable, even by Moses himself. "Moses was not able to enter the tent of meeting because the cloud settled on it, and the glory of the LORD filled the tabernacle."

Though we desire communion and fellowship with God, every natural inclination of our heart resists him. We are unable to come near to him. He is life; we are mortal. He is pure; we are polluted. He is infinite; we are finite. He is holy; we are common. He is transcendent; we are not. Man cannot, on his own, enter his Presence.

The end of Exodus leaves the reader with a cliffhanger: How are the Israelites supposed to approach God? How are they to come near to him? If Moses, who stood in the LORD's presence on Mount Sinai, could not enter, how much less the ordinary person?

Korban: A Gift Brought Near

The book of Leviticus answers the question that Exodus left unanswered.

> The LORD called Moses and spoke to him from the tent of meeting, saying, "Speak to the people of Israel and say to them, 'When any one of you brings an *offering* to the LORD, you shall bring your *offering* of livestock from the herd or from the flock.'" (Leviticus 1:1–2)

The word "offering" translates the Hebrew word *korban* (קרבן). It's a "sacrifice." Neither of those English words accurately expresses the concept. The word "sacrifice" implies that the person bringing it must deprive himself of something he cherishes. The word "offering" implies a payment, a fee, a tribute, or gratuity. But God has no satisfaction in inflicting deprivation upon his children, and he is not in need of tribute or gifts.

The word *korban* implies more than merely a sacrifice or an offering. The root of the word *korban* is *karav,* (קרב), a Hebrew verbal root that can be translated "to come near." A *korban* could be defined as, "something brought near." The person bringing a *korban* does so in order to come closer to God.

The first verses of Leviticus imply that man himself cannot "come near" to God in his dwelling place, the Tabernacle (or Temple). God is holy; he is other; he is distinct and separate from man. Therefore, man must send a substitute in his place. He sends a *korban* as a vehicle that allows him to draw near to God in the holy place. If we understand a *korban* as "something brought near," we might paraphrase the first passage of Leviticus as follows:

> When any one of you wants to draw near with something brought near to the LORD, you shall *bring near your thing brought near* of livestock from the herd or from the flock. (Leviticus 1:1–2)

To "draw near" to God in his holy place is to enter communion with the manifest presence of God on earth. In as much as his presence resided in the Tabernacle on earth, the worshipper was able to draw near and enter into that presence through the offering of a *korban*—something brought near.

To put it another way, the Hebrew word *korban* could be translated as "gift." The Israelites were to view the sacrifices as gifts that they could bring to God.

Does God need these gifts? Of course not. In Psalm 50 he declares that he owns every beast and the cattle on a thousand hills. He says, "If I were hungry, I would not tell you, for the world and its fullness are mine. Do I eat the flesh of bulls or drink the blood of goats?" He does not need sacrifices any more than he needs our prayers or our songs of praise, but all three are things that he has enabled human beings to offer to him so that they can enjoy relationship with him.

Of course, not all sacrifices can be thought of as voluntary gifts. Some sacrifices, such as the sin offerings, are mandated. A sacrifice like that should be thought of as tribute exacted by a great king, whereas the voluntary sacrifices are like gifts presented to the king by his loyal subjects.

Appeasing an Angry God

This explanation presents a different understanding of sacrifice than we are ordinarily taught. We are normally taught that the children of Israel brought sacrifices to pay the penalty for their sins. By this reasoning, the sacrifices function as a sort of scapegoat. When a man merited the divine death penalty at the hands of heaven, he could make a sacrifice instead. He slaughtered the unfortunate cow or sheep or goat in his place.

An oversimplification of this concept has it that God was angry with the sinner and demanded punishment, even the sinner's death. After all, the wages of sin are death. The sinner then killed an animal, and the death of the animal appeased God. God no longer felt angry after the animal was sacrificed. At least something had been killed! The blood of the animal appeased the angry God.

Is this really what the Torah teaches? Is this really what the apostles taught? No, not entirely. Sacrificial substitution and propitiation are far more complex and mystical. Furthermore, most of the sacrifices were not offered for sin at all. It is true that the Torah does require "sin offerings" and "guilt offerings" for certain sins and failings, but most of the sacrifices described in the Bible are not like that. Instead, in most cases, a glad, willing worshipper offers his sacrifices voluntarily—not as a ransom for life.

Sacrifice as Payment for Sin

Christians often think that in Old Testament times people had to bring sacrifices to pay for their sins. The sacrifices, for the most part, are not about paying for sin. In Torah, the death of the animal does not substitute for the death of the sinner. Instead, the death of the animal provides a proxy to bring the worshipper near to God. It does not appease an angry God. It provides a method by which God might be approached.

Nevertheless, they do illustrate the concept of "vicarious suffering and atonement." Vicarious suffering and atonement means that someone else suffers on your behalf and provides atonement for you. The animal sacrifices also teach important lessons about life and death. They graphically illustrate sin and punishment. They teach us that entering into the presence of the holy God is a costly affair—not something entered into haphazardly or casually. Blood must be shed to effect communion with God. The great rabbi, Nachmanides, understood the sacrificial service in exactly those terms. He suggested that as the animal underwent slaughter, the offerer should be thinking that he himself deserved to be slaughtered. As the priests splashed the animal's blood on the altar, the offerer should be thinking that his own blood should be spilled in consequence for his sin.

Sacrifice implies that we stand in debt to God. The grand words of propitiation, redemption, and atonement all communicate an aspect of repayment. Even when the sacrifices are voluntary, the death of the sacrificial victim is a central issue.

Still, sacrifices are not primarily about paying for one's sins.

Five Types of Sacrifice

The first seven chapters of Leviticus list and describe five different major categories of sacrifices. Each of these categories contains many variations. All the sacrifices in the Bible fall into one of these five classes. The next two chapters will provide a brief overview of each type of sacrifice.

Common English Name	Hebrew Name	Scripture
Burnt Offering	*Olah* עולה	Leviticus 1:1–17; 6:8–13
Grain Offering	*Minchah* מנחה	Leviticus 2:1–16; 6:14–23
Peace Offering	*Shelami* שלמים	Leviticus 3:1–17; 7:11–36
Sin Offering	*Chatat* חטאת	Leviticus 4:1–5:13; 6:24–7:7
Guilt Offering	*Asham* אשם	Leviticus 5:14–6:7; 7:1–7

Summary

The Israelites built the Tabernacle as the dwelling place of God on earth, but that did not solve the problem of how Israel could approach a holy God. The word *korban* (sacrifice) derives from the root *karav*, meaning "to draw near." God does not need our sacrifices; rather we need to draw near to him. Two misconceptions of sacrifices are that they are either to appease an angry God or to pay for sin. The five main categories of sacrifices are: burnt offerings, grain offerings, peace offerings, sin offerings, and guilt offerings. Only the last two are specifically concerned with sin.

Questions

1. What problem does the book of Exodus leave unresolved?
2. The root of *korban* (usually translated as "sacrifice") is *karav*, which means what?
3. Discuss: The sacrifices were not designed to appease an angry God.
4. Discuss: The sacrifices were not all designed as payments for sin.
5. Name the five basic types of sacrifices in the Torah.

2
Sacrificial Basics

> If his offering is a burnt offering from the herd, he shall offer a male without blemish. He shall bring it to the entrance of the tent of meeting, that he may be accepted before the LORD. (Leviticus 1:3)

The priestly laws of Leviticus introduce five categories of sacrifices, beginning with the most fundamental and basic of all, the "burnt offering." By studying the laws that pertain to a burnt offering, we will learn principles that apply to all types of Levitical sacrifices.

The English name "burnt offering" does not accurately translate the Hebrew: *korban olah* (קרבן עלה). The word *olah* means "that which rises." The *korban olah* could be called "a sacrifice that rises."

The worshipper who brought an animal as an *olah* offering completely surrendered it to God. The ancient Israelite had nothing to gain by offering an *olah*. He did not bring an *olah* offering to compensate for sin or guilt. Unlike the other types of sacrifices that a worshipper might bring to the LORD, the *olah* did not profit the worshipper in any way. He retained no choice cuts of meat. He received no ritual purification from the *olah*, no expiation, nothing but complete giving over to God. The fire on the altar consumed the entire animal. The very word *olah* suggests this: "that which rises." The altar fire translated the substance of the sacrifice into heat and smoke which "rise" to heaven as a sweet savor before the LORD.

More than any other *korban* that might be presented to the Lord, the *olah* symbolizes a complete and total surrender to God. It stands in the stead of its owner as a token of complete, selfless devotion of one's entire essence—a reckless abandonment to God. In that respect, the *olah* symbolizes the total *tzadik* (righteous person); he completely surrenders his will and essence to God as a "living sacrifice, holy and acceptable to God" (Romans 12:1). Such is the Master, the living *korban olah* of the eternal altar.

A Voluntary Act of Worship

Ordinarily (but not always), a man brought an *olah* voluntarily. He brought it because he desired to draw near to God. Jewish tradition teaches that the *olah* could only be brought with great joy of heart. An animal offered reluctantly was not considered to be a proper sacrifice.

The same rule applies to all of the voluntary offerings. The worshipper was to bring the sacrifice in joyful heart and gladness. For example, in Psalm 27:6 David exclaims, "I will offer in his tent sacrifices with shouts of joy; I will sing and make melody to the LORD."

The people of Israel viewed sacrifice as a joyous rite. They considered it a privilege and eagerly sought to participate in the rituals. They accompanied their sacrifices with music, song, prayer, and worship. The book of Psalms contains many songs composed to accompany various sacrifices. The man bringing the *olah* found fulfillment and communion with God through the ritual. His soul was happy; his heart beat with expectation as he brought his animal to the Temple.

Like the *olah,* most sacrifices were not brought as a punishment for sin, but out of a glad heart which sought to "come near" to God. This is the biblical perspective on true worship.

A Ritual Surrogate

The worshipper regarded the sacrificial animal as a substitute for himself. He offered it at "the entrance of the tent of meeting, that he may be accepted before the LORD." In that respect, the sacrifice was a ritual surrogate for the offerer.

The Torah explains, "He shall lay his hand on the head of the burnt offering, and it shall be accepted for him" (Leviticus 1:4). The first ritual procedure in offering any animal *korban* (excepting birds) was the laying on of hands (*semichah*, סמיכה). The act of *semichah* implied a physical "leaning" on the animal so that the weight of the man was transferred to the animal, symbolizing an investment of identity.

The same terminology is used in Numbers 8:10 where all Israel laid their hands upon the Levites to designate them as surrogates. In Numbers 27 God commanded Moses to lay his hands on Joshua, thereby appointing Joshua as the new leader of Israel. Through laying his hands on Joshua, Moses invested him with his authority, and Joshua became Moses' substitute.

In Judaism, judges, elders, and rabbis were ordained through the ritual of laying on of hands. In the Apostolic Scriptures, Yeshua and the apostles sometimes conferred healing by the laying on of hands. The apostles conferred the Holy Spirit by laying on of hands. They ordained elders and deacons through the laying on of hands. They considered laying on of hands as one of the elementary doctrines of the Messianic faith.[1]

In each of these instances, the laying on of hands symbolizes a transfer of identity. Through the laying on of hands, the one leaning confers his identity onto the one being leaned upon. The Levites are invested with the identity of all Israel. Joshua is invested with the identity of Moses. Judges, elders, rabbis, and deacons transfer their authority and office to new judges, elders, rabbis, and deacons through the laying on of hands.

When a man leaned his hands on the head of an animal, he invested his identity into the animal. The animal then represented him before the LORD. In the case of sin offerings, a man confessed his sins while laying his hands on the animal.

Atonement

The Torah instructed the worshipper to "lay his hand on the head of the burnt offering, and it shall be accepted for him to make atonement for him" (Leviticus 1:4). One might assume that the sacrifice was meant as an atonement for sin, but this is not accurate.

The Torah's use of the term atonement (*kaphar*, כפר) certainly can imply the forgiveness of sin and removal of guilt, but the word meant more than that. In the story of Noah's ark, the Torah uses the word *kaphar* to mean the application of a protective covering. When the Torah describes how Noah applied pitch to the exterior of his ark, it uses the term *kaphar*. "Cover (*kaphar*, כפר) it inside and out with pitch" (Genesis 6:14). The Torah also uses a form of the word *kaphar* as "ransom" for one's life. Both of the meanings apply in the ritual context of Israel's worship system.

In the Torah's instructions for the building of the Tabernacle, the priesthood, the altar, the furnishings, and even the Tabernacle itself, all required *kaphar* in the sense of "covering." They all need to be covered in order to stand in the presence of God. Without such covering, they would not survive the encounter with the consuming Spirit of the Almighty.

The same was also true for the worshipper that sought to "draw near" to God's manifest presence within his holy place. God is dangerous, and to be near him in the flesh is to be in jeopardy. The sacrificial system was a means by which those who desired to draw near to his manifest presence could do so safely, albeit through the agency of surrogates. Fragile, mortal flesh might not survive his presence. The man must send a surrogate on his behalf. In view of those concerns, we should understand Levitical atonement primarily as a covering in the sense of a protective shelter from the manifest presence of God, who occupied the Temple.

Sacrifice for Salvation?

In the sacrificial context, "atonement" does not mean attainment of salvation. The people did not bring sacrifices to attain salvation. A sinner did not bring a sacrifice to clear his conscience, and he did not bring a sacrifice to acquire forgiveness for his intentional sins. The writer of the book of Hebrews makes it quite clear that the sacrifices were not intended to remove sin or regenerate the sinner when he says, "For it is impossible for the blood of bulls and goats to take away sins" (Hebrews 10:4). In another place he explains that the sacrifices could not cleanse the conscience because they were only intended to relate to matters of the flesh (i.e., the physical body), not the spirit (i.e., the divine soul):

> Gifts and sacrifices are offered that cannot perfect the
> conscience of the worshipper, but deal only with food

and drink and various washings, regulations for the body. (Hebrews 9:9–10)

Believers misunderstand the sacrificial system because they view it through the grid of "Old Covenant" and "New Covenant" theology. We make the mistake of assuming that prior to the death and resurrection of our Master, people procured forgiveness and salvation through their participation in the sacrificial rites. We thereby assign to the rites of animal sacrifice efficacy unto eternal salvation—up until the Master's death. But if this were actually true, then he need not have died at all. Rather his sacrifice and death become simply a matter of convenience for us. According to this theology, it is convenient that we no longer need to offer animal sacrifices, but if not for Yeshua, they would suffice us.

What was God's intention for the sacrifices if not for forgiveness and salvation? It is hard for us to understand this, because the Temple is no longer standing. One can no longer enter a holy space occupied by the manifest presence of God. If such a place still existed, we would better understand the need for atonement as it pertains to God's presence in this world. The sacrifices and Temple rituals pertained to drawing near to God within his holy precincts. They were rituals for the Temple in this present world. The writer of Hebrews makes this clear with a *kal vachomer* (קל וחומר) argument, i.e., *a minori ad maius,* a common method of rabbinic argumentation where one reasons from the light to the heavy: "If such and such is true, how much more so is such and such true." He argues that if animal sacrifices were efficacious as regards the flesh, how much more so is the sacrifice of Messiah as regards the spirit.

> For if the blood of goats and bulls, and the sprinkling of defiled persons with the ashes of a heifer, sanctify for the purification of the flesh, how much more will the blood of Christ, who through the eternal Spirit offered himself without blemish to God, purify our conscience from dead works to serve the living God? (Hebrews 9:13–14)

The Temple sacrifices sanctified for the cleansing of the flesh, but they did nothing to cleanse the spirit (i.e., the divine soul that lives on after death). That could only be accomplished by faith and repentance. Likewise, the sages say, "neither the sin offering, nor the guilt offering, nor the Day of Atonement can bring expiation without repentance" (t.*Yoma* 5:9).

The Soul in the Blood

How did sacrificing bring the Israelite near to God? How did the sacrifices work? A brief examination of the sacrificial blood ritual reveals the symbolic, spiritual mechanics at work. Leviticus 1:5 describes the blood transaction:

> Then he shall kill the bull before the LORD, and Aaron's sons the priests shall bring the blood and throw the blood against the sides of the altar that is at the entrance of the tent of meeting.

The offerer, not the priest, did the actual slaying of the animal. A priest oversaw the slaughter and caught the animal's blood in a basin. The priest then carried the blood to the altar and splashed it on the four sides of the altar.

In the Torah, blood contains the living soul of a creature. Whether human or animal, we all possess a living essence. The Torah refers to this life-force as our *nefesh* (נפש), a word we translate as "soul," but it does not necessarily mean the divine soul that lives on after death (*neshamah*, נשמה). The *nefesh* can simply refer to the spark of life which animates our flesh. It is our person, personality, our identity in the flesh. The mystics call it the *nefesh chayah*, i.e., the "animal soul." The blood can be said to contain this soul, because when one's blood is spilled from his body, his life leaves with it. In that respect, the Torah uses the word *nefesh* the way we sometimes use the word "life."

> For the life (*nefesh*) of the flesh is in the blood, and I have given it for you on the altar to make atonement for your souls (*nefesh*), for it is the blood that makes atonement by the life (*nefesh*). (Leviticus 17:11)

As the priest splashed the animal's blood upon the altar, he actually applied the animal's *nefesh* to the altar, because the *nefesh* is in the blood. Because of the laying-on-of-hands ritual, the LORD regarded the animal's blood—its soul—as the worshipper's. That is to say, in God's eyes, the priest splashed the blood of the man bringing the sacrifice on the altar. In God's eyes, the *nefesh* of the man was applied to the altar.

Watch the whole process. The worshipper selected a kosher, unblemished animal and then, through the laying on of hands, he invested his identity onto the animal. Once the animal was legally recognized as bearing the worshipper's identity, the man slaughtered it in order to draw out the soul with the blood. The priest caught the blood/soul of the animal in a basin; however, the animal's blood now represented the worshipper's life. The priest then carried the blood/soul to the altar and applied it there.

The Meaning of an Altar

In the ancient world, people considered altars as touching points between heaven and earth. An altar worked like a gate, a sort of mystical portal between the realm of man and the realm of the divine. Whatever touched the altar became holy (ritually set apart) to God and entered his presence.

From on top of the altar, the bodies of the sacrifices ascended in smoke to God. Through the medium of the animal's blood, the offerer's soul entered the presence of God. In short, the soul of the worshipper came near to God in his holy place. The sacrificial substitute overcame the problem of approaching a holy God.

According to this interpretation, the death of the animal was not the purpose of sacrifice. The *korban* was about life, not death. The sacrifice was about the life and soul of the animal. The death of the animal only provided the means by which the blood/soul might be procured for use in the blood ritual.

All of this presents a very different interpretation of sacrifice than the traditional ones, which tell us that the death of the sacrifice atones for the sinner. However, in the Torah we see that it was not the death, but the life—the soul and the blood of the animal—which brought the unworthy mortal close to God. Jewish believer and Temple scholar Alfred Edersheim points out, "The death of the sacrifice was only a means towards an end, that end being the shedding and sprinkling of the blood, by which the atonement was really made."[2]

Again, the death of the animal accomplished nothing for the man. The animal's death provided no atonement or communion. Those things existed in the life, the blood of the animal. Sacrifice is about life, not death.

A Soothing Aroma

> And the priest shall offer up in smoke all of it on the altar
> for a burnt offering, an offering by fire of a soothing aroma
> to the LORD. (Leviticus 1:9)

As the Torah describes the sacrificial service, it says that the priest shall burn the body of the sacrifice on the altar. When the smoke of the offering rises to heaven, the LORD receives it as a "soothing (or pleasing) aroma." At first this seems strange. Does God really like the smell of burning meat?

Rabbi Shlomo ben Yitzchak (Rashi) interprets the "pleasing aroma" as a metaphor for man's obedience. He explains that the aroma of the sacrifice brings pleasure to the LORD because it is a token of his children's obedience. When God "smells" the aroma of the sacrifice, he says, "I have given commandments and my will has been obeyed."[3] "To obey is better than sacrifice, and to listen than the fat of rams" (1 Samuel 15:22).

In the same line of thought, the pleasing aroma of the sacrifice symbolizes God's acceptance of man's gift. Remember that the sacrifices are intended as ritual gifts to the Almighty. When God "smells" the sacrifice, he delights in the human being who comes to draw near to him.

Regardless of how we understand it, the Torah makes it clear that God took delight in the sacrifices. He graciously accepted the gifts of his people, and the smoke that rose from the altar fires was as a pleasing aroma to him.

Doesn't God Hate the Sacrifices?

This might seem difficult to reconcile with many statements in the prophets where God speaks out against the sacrifices. For example, in the book of Isaiah he says, "I have had enough of burnt offerings of rams and the fat of well-fed beasts; I do not delight in the blood of bulls, or of lambs, or of goats ... bring no more vain offerings" (Isaiah 1:11–13). Likewise, in the book of Jeremiah he says, "Your burnt offerings are not acceptable, nor your sacrifices pleasing to me" (Jeremiah 6:20). In the book of Malachi he says, "[If only] you might not kindle fire on my altar in vain! ... I will not accept an offering from your hand" (Malachi 1:10). In the early days of Christianity, the church fathers often cited texts like these, trying to prove that God had never wanted the sacrificial system. Some suggested, from these and similar passages, that God had given the sacrifices to the Jews as a punishment. They argued against the Jewish people, claiming that Jesus had done away with the sacrifices because God had always hated them.

That does not make sense. If God always hated the sacrifices, why did he command the children of Israel to bring them in the first place? Why did he state over and over that he was pleased with them?

A better explanation comes from a more careful reading of the prophets. When the prophets seem to speak against the sacrificial system, they are not condemning the mode of worship; they are condemning the worshippers. In every instance the prophets direct their rebuke toward the immoral, disobedient people among the Israelites who violated the covenant of Torah while continuing to go through the motions of the sacrificial system. Though their hearts were far from God, they continued to perform their religious rituals.

This can be compared to a wicked womanizer who beats his wife and cheats on her but continues to faithfully attend church every Sunday and take communion with the rest of the congregation. His religious ritual is meaningless and an insult to God. Or suppose the same fellow, after beating his wife and cheating on her, sends her a bouquet of roses to compensate. Would she be pleased to receive the flowers? Hardly. She would say, "Your flowers are an abomination to me!" In the same way, God hates religious rituals when they are performed hypocritically.

These lessons should be a warning to all of us. We must be careful not to develop any sense of right-standing with God because of ritual observances. God is interested in the state of our hearts. Our outward rituals should reflect our inward conditions.

Messiah: The Means to Draw Near

We all desire to "draw near" to God. Yet human sin and mortality cuts us off from communion and fellowship with him. We are unable to approach the holy God. Just as Moses was unable to enter the Tabernacle at the end of the book of Exodus, we too are unable to enter into God's presence. He is holy; we are common. He is immortal; we are mortal. He is pure; we are impure. He is righteousness; we are sinful. We cannot come near to God without a *korban* (something brought near) in our stead.

The Torah told the children of Israel to bring an unblemished animal for a *korban*. The sacrificed *korban* vicariously brought the worshipper into the presence of God. As regards the eternal Temple above, the Master is our *korban*. He is the unblemished, perfect, and sinless one that brings us near and into the presence of God. No man comes to the Father except through Yeshua.

By confessing his name and entering his salvation, we identify with him, much as a man who laid his hands upon his *korban* identified with the sacrificial animal. We are to identify with our Master to the extent that we consider ourselves to have died and risen with him. Much as the officiating priest carried the sacrificial blood to the altar, the Master bears his own life to the heavenly altar, and through his blood he brings us near to his Father.

To "draw near" to God is to enter into communion with him; it implies entering his very presence. Inasmuch as his presence resided in the Tabernacle and Temple on earth, the worshipper was able to draw near and enter into that presence through the offering of a *korban*—something brought near.

Though the worshipper was able to draw near to God within the Temple on Earth through means of the sacrificial blood of animals, such blood never availed to bring him near to God in the eternal sense of life after death and the world to come. Though the blood of the bull allowed him to draw near to God's presence in the earthly Tabernacle, it did not avail him the same privilege in the true Temple in heaven. The Master brings us near to God in the heavenly Temple:

> It can never, by the same sacrifices that are continually offered every year, make perfect those who draw near. Otherwise, would they not have ceased to be offered, since

the worshipers, having once been cleansed, would no longer have any consciousness of sins? (Hebrews 10:1–2)

For the law made nothing perfect; but on the other hand, a better hope is introduced, through which we <u>draw near</u> to God. (Hebrews 7:19)

Consequently, he is able to save to the uttermost those who <u>draw near</u> to God through him, since he always lives to make intercession for them. (Hebrews 7:25)

Let us then with confidence <u>draw near</u> to the throne of grace, that we may receive mercy and find grace to help us in our time of need. (Hebrews 4:16)

Let us <u>draw near</u> with a true heart in full assurance of faith, with our hearts sprinkled clean from an evil conscience and our bodies washed with pure water. (Hebrews 10:22)

A Different Interpretation

It is true that the Master took upon himself the punishment for our sin, i.e., death. However, he accomplished more than that. He is more than a scapegoat for us. More than simply taking our punishment, Yeshua brings us into the presence of his Father. That is a function of his life! The death of Yeshua would have availed nothing had he not risen. In his rising, his conquest over death, he brings us near to his Father. Had Yeshua not risen, he would have been as a sacrifice slaughtered but not brought to the altar. His death then, was a necessary means toward an end, that end being the shedding and sprinkling of the blood by which he made atonement. In other words, it is the life of the living Messiah that brings us near to God.

Summary

The worshipper who brings a burnt offering (*olah*) completely surrenders his sacrifice to God without expecting any tangible reward; the burnt offering is like the *tzadik*, a person wholly surrendered to God. The worshipper, glad to commune with God, brings the offering voluntarily. He lays hands on the sacrificial animal, transferring his identity to it, and the animal represents him to the LORD. It becomes a "covering" for him as he approaches God. Hebrews tells us that the sacrifices did not atone in the sense of bringing salvation; rather they "cleansed the flesh." The animal's blood was its life and represented the worshipper's life. The sacrifices are a "soothing aroma" to God, who delights in the love and obedience of worshippers. God did not hate Israel's sacrifices as such; rather he hated the religious rites of those who persisted in sin. There are many parallels between Messiah's work and the sacrifices.

Questions

1. In the phrase *korban olah* (usually translated "burnt offering"), what does *olah* mean?
2. What benefit did the worshipper receive from a voluntary burnt offering?
3. What is the significance of the worshipper laying his hand on the sacrificial animal?
4. Atonement (*kaphar*) does not always mean the removal of sin and guilt. Explain the concept of atonement in the Levitical sense.
5. Discuss: Atonement (in the Temple) does not mean attaining salvation.
6. Discuss: The Temple sacrifices served for the "cleansing of the flesh."
7. Discuss: It is the life, not the death, of the animal that atones.
8. What did an altar represent to ancient people?
9. Why did the prophets say, at times, that God hated Israel's sacrifices?

3
Other Sacrifices

In the previous chapter, we learned about burnt offerings, only one of the five types of sacrifices described in the opening chapters of Leviticus. In this chapter, we will briefly examine the other four major types of sacrifices: the grain offering, the peace offering, the sin offering, and the guilt offering.

The Grain Offerings

All of the sacrifices and offerings are best understood as ritual gifts given to God by which the worshipper was able to draw near to the LORD in his holy place. The first chapter of Leviticus described the *korban olah* gift, the "burnt offering." The second chapter of Leviticus describes a second type of gift, the "grain offering."

> When anyone brings a grain offering as an offering to the
> LORD, his offering shall be of fine flour. He shall pour oil
> on it and put frankincense on it. (Leviticus 2:1)

The term "grain offering" is a descriptive but not a literal translation of the Hebrew term *minchah* (מנחה). English translators refer to the *minchah* as a grain offering because it consisted primarily of flour from wheat or barley. Some older English versions of the Bible translate *minchah* as the "meal offering" or "cereal offering." Ironically, the King James Version translates it as "meat offering" (King James readers, beware! There was no meat in that meat offering. The grain offering was the only vegan sacrifice in Leviticus, so why does the King James Version call it the "meat offering?" In King James

English, the word "meat" did not mean "flesh" as it does in modern English. The word "meat" referred to food in general.)

The Hebrew word *minchah* does not literally mean either grain offering or meat offering. Like the word *korban,* the word *minchah* means "gift" or "tribute." Therefore, the grain offerings should be translated as "gift offerings." (Jewish terminology also refers to the time of afternoon prayer as *minchah,* because the three times of prayer originally corresponded to Temple's sacrificial services.)

Like a burnt offering, the *minchah* offering was not a penalty for sin. A worshipper brought a grain offering as a freewill gift to God, completely voluntary.

The grain offering consisted primarily of grain (usually as wheat flour), oil, and frankincense. The grain offering proves that the Levitical sacrifices did all not die on behalf of sinners. How could flour die on someone's behalf? Instead, the priests offered a small handful of the grain offering on the altar and ate the rest of it.

Unleavened and Salted

Like the *matzah* at Passover, the priests prepared the grain offerings unleavened. In the Temple, leaven and fermentation symbolized corruption, decay, and mortality.

The LORD received the grain offerings baked in an oven, fried in a pan, deep-pan fried, or left uncooked. Worshippers brought grain offerings to the altar in conjunction with other types of sacrifices, like burnt offerings and peace offerings. Poor people who could not afford animals for sacrifice brought grain offerings instead.

The Torah required every grain offering to be seasoned with salt before being placed upon the altar, in order to symbolize "the salt of the covenant with your God" (Leviticus 2:13). People in the ancient world used salt as a preservative. The "salt of the covenant" refers to the unchanging and eternal nature of God's covenant with Israel. Just as salt kept foods from turning rancid, God's faithfulness preserves his covenant with his people. To this day, at every Shabbat table, the observant Jewish family dashes a little salt on the Sabbath bread or dips the bread into salt before eating it, because the Talmud says, "A man's table is like the altar" (b.*Berachot* 55a).

Peace Offerings

The third chapter of Leviticus introduces the third major classification of sacrifice: the peace offering.

> If his offering is a sacrifice of peace offering, if he offers an animal from the herd, male or female, he shall offer it without blemish before the LORD. (Leviticus 3:1)

The term "peace offerings" translates the Hebrew word *shelamim* (שלמים). They are called peace offerings because the word *shelamim* is related to *shalom* (שלום) which means "peace."

Like the burnt offering and the grain offering, worshippers brought peace offerings voluntarily. Many different types of sacrifices fall into the peace offering category. Thanksgiving offerings, votive offerings, freewill offerings, and Passover lambs were all peace offerings—sacrifices in which the one bringing the animal partook. Peace offerings were never brought as a penalty for sin or to earn forgiveness for sin.

Like the burnt offering, the peace offering had to be an unblemished animal from the herd or the flock, but unlike the burnt offering, the priests only burned the animal's choice fats on the altar: "the fat covering the entrails and all the fat that is on the entrails, and the two kidneys with the fat that is on them at the loins, and the long lobe of the liver" (Leviticus 3:3–4). The priesthood divided the rest of the sacrifice between the person who brought the peace offering and the priest who offered it on the altar. The peace offering created an opportunity for the worshipper to share in the table of the LORD. It symbolized a shared meal between the worshipper who brought the sacrifice, the priesthood, and God himself. The peace offering represented peace and mutual goodwill between God and the worshipper. It represented fellowship between God and man.

The meat of the peace offering was to be used for a fellowship meal. The man who sacrificed a peace offering invited his whole family, his friends, and his acquaintances to partake of the sacrificial meats. Any Israelite in a state of ritual purity could eat from it. Most people sacrificed peace offerings in conjunction with the festivals. Families travelled together to Jerusalem, offered their peace offerings, and then enjoyed them together as a component of keeping

God's appointed times. Maybe that's where the tradition of big festival meals comes from.

What about Sin?

So far we have learned three of the five types of offerings, but none of them were penalties for sin. People did not offer burnt offerings, grain offerings, or peace offerings to pay for sins. They brought them to the LORD in his holy dwelling place as ritual gifts that a person could give to God out of a glad and willing heart.

The remaining two types of sacrifices, however, are concerned with sin: the sin offering and the guilt offering.

Before discussing the sin offering and the guilt offering, however, we should take note of how the Torah defines sin. The Torah says that a person sins when he does "any of the things which the LORD has commanded not to be done" (Leviticus 4:2, NASB). The converse is also true. A sin is failure to do anything the LORD has commanded to be done. To put it simply, sin is breaking God's commandments.

"Sin" means to "miss the mark." It is based on the Hebrew root *chata* (חטא), an archery term. A sin is like an arrow that falls short of its intended target, as Paul says, "For all have sinned and fall short of the glory of God" (Romans 3:23). The word *Torah* also derives from an archery term. The word *yarah* (ירה), the verbal root of *Torah* (תורה), means "to take aim." Just as an archer aims for a target, a man practicing righteousness aims for the mark of Torah. When he fails to fulfill the Torah, he falls short of the target, and that's what "sin" means. The Torah says that even an unintentional transgression of God's commandments is a sin.

The Bible teaches that sin is a condition common to all men. Paul says, "All have sinned" (Romans 3:23). The book of Ecclesiastes says, "Surely there is not a righteous man on earth who does good and never sins" (Ecclesiastes 7:20). The Torah seems to illustrate the same concept here, assuming that not only the common people sin, but also the king, the elders, and even the anointed holy priest.

Knowing that everyone sins, it might be tempting to wink at one's own moral failings, to shrug and say, "Oh, well, no one's perfect; everyone sins."

The laws of the sin offerings illustrate the gravity of sin. Disobedience to God's commandments is a serious matter, not something to be discarded with a cavalier attitude. Even unintentional sins are regarded as so serious that a sacrifice must be brought to repair the relationship.

Sin Offerings

The fourth chapter of Leviticus says that when a man sins unintentionally, he should bring a sin offering to the LORD. It does not tell us what a man should do if he sins intentionally. The Torah did not want to create the impression that a man could buy the freedom to intentionally commit a sin by having a sin offering ready.

The Hebrew word translated as "sin offering" (*chatat,* חטאת) looks almost identical to the word for "sin" (*cheit,* חטא). Depending on who sinned, the Torah prescribes several different types of sin offerings. If the high priest sins, he must bring a bull. If the whole community sins, the elders representing the community must bring a bull. If a leader of the community (such as the king) sins, he must bring a male goat. If an Israelite sins, he must bring a female goat or lamb. If he cannot afford the goat or lamb, he can bring a pair of doves. If he cannot afford the doves, he can bring flour as a type of sin offering. The ritual procedures for the sin offerings differ depending on which type is brought.

However, the sin offering was not a penalty for sinning. Instead, it was a means of spiritual purification after sin had been confessed, repented of, and forgiven. The sin offering was not brought only for sin. As with the other sacrifices, the sin offering was a type of gift to God. It did not earn forgiveness, but it was an appropriate gesture to make. Sin offerings were also brought in connection with ritual purification.

There are several instances when a sin offering must be brought even though there is no sin committed. For example, each of the following was required to bring a sin offering, even though he or she had not sinned:

- A woman after childbirth. (Leviticus 12:6)
- A leper after his cleansing. (Leviticus 14:19)

- A Nazarite who came into contact with a corpse. (Numbers 6:11)
- A Nazarite who completed the term of his vow. (Numbers 6:14)

None of these people actually committed a sin. Therefore, the *chatat* should not be understood to be simply an offering for sin. A better conceptual translation for the *chatat* might be "purification offering." The Hebrew word *chata* sometimes denotes a purification instead of a sin. For example, "Moses took the blood, and with his finger put it on the horns of the altar around it and purified (*chata*, חטא) the altar" (Leviticus 8:15). Likewise, the Torah calls the ashes of the red heifer which are used to ritually purify a person contaminated by contact with a human corpse a "sin offering," but they are for ceremonial purification, not for cleansing from sin. The Torah also tells the priests to sprinkle the blood of sin offerings in many of the purification rituals.

This makes a good deal of sense. A *chatat* is often mandated for an individual that has become ritually unclean. The unclean person has not sinned, but he or she is in need of purification. Understanding a *chatat* as a "purification offering" instead of only a "sin offering" resolves the difficulties and helps us better understand the rituals involved.

The Guilt Offering

The fifth chapter of Leviticus introduces the fifth type of sacrifice: the guilt offering. In most respects, the guilt offering is similar to the sin offering, and it can be considered as a specific type of sin offering.

The Hebrew word *asham* (אשם), which we translate as "guilt offering," implies indemnity and reparation. The Torah prescribes a guilt offering primarily for offenses that require a payment of restitution. It seems to be a type of repayment offering. When a person committed a sin, like misappropriation of someone else's property or the misuse of sacred objects, the Torah required him to pay reparations and to bring a guilt offering. The Torah says that he had to repay the full amount of damages plus one fifth, and then bring a guilt offering to the LORD.

The laws of the guilt offering teach that an offense toward another person is also an offense against God. When we cheat or damage or misuse others or their property, it is as if we have cheated, damaged, and misused God. Therefore, when we settle accounts, we must repay both the victim and God. The victim receives the full value of his property plus one fifth; the LORD receives the *asham,* the guilt offering.

The Torah does not say that the sacrifice takes away the sin, but it does say that if a man confesses the sin, repents, makes reparation, and seeks atonement before the LORD, "he shall be forgiven for any of the things that one may do and thereby become guilty" in misusing either another person's property or sacred property (Leviticus 6:7).

Lessons from the Sacrifices

We have only summarized and, in some cases, oversimplified the five types of sacrifices. Nevertheless, even this superficial overview of the sacrifices has revealed several critical truths:

- The different types of sacrifices have different meanings.
- Not all of the sacrifices are sin offerings.
- The sacrifices were a means for drawing near to the inapproachable God within his holy Temple on earth.
- Most of the sacrifices are more like gifts than penalties.

Studying the sacrifices also reminds us that the God we worship does not always fit well into our conception of what he should be like. The God of the Bible is a God who took delight in the slaughter of sacrificial animals and who described the smoke that rose from his altar fires as a pleasing aroma. Though he certainly had no need of their tribute, he invited his people to serve him with gifts by slaughtering bulls, goats, and rams.

The sacrificial system reminds us that the God of the Bible is a strange and untamed God, utterly holy and removed. He is so completely other that one who wanted to enter into his holy Tabernacle could only do so by means of the sacrifices. Moreover, human sin, even if inadvertent, so grieves God that it cannot be left unaddressed. An unintentional sin required a sin offering, and a sin against another person required both reparation and sacrifice. Who has a chance of standing in judgment before such an exacting God? The good news is that through the atoning death of God's Son, we can be washed of sin, cleansed, and forgiven.

Summary

The *minchah* offerings are primarily of grain; the word means "gift" or "tribute." Part of the grain was burned on the altar, while the priests ate the rest. People too poor to offer animals could substitute grain. The "peace" or goodwill offerings, *shelamim*, were also voluntary. In them, meat from the sacrificed animal was shared by the priest and by the worshipper, his family, and friends. The sin and guilt offerings served to restore relationship with God, following violation of commandments or contraction of ritual impurity. Realizing that God commanded the offering of sacrifices and that the sacrificial system pleased him should make us realize that he is not as we might imagine him.

Questions

1. Discuss: The sacrifices and offerings are best understood as ritual gifts given to God by which the worshipper was able to draw near to the LORD in his holy place.

2. What is the non-animal sacrifice in Leviticus 2?

3. The word for the grain offering, *minchah*, literally means what?

4. What does salt on the sacrifices symbolize?

5. With "peace offerings" (*shelamim*), parts of the animal were burned on the altar, a part went to the priest, and what happened with the rest?

6. Discuss sin as *chata*, "missing the mark," and the Torah as *yarah*, "to aim."

7. Sin and guilt offerings served for unintentional sin and ritual impurity. What was the sacrifice for willful sin?

ing to the Torah, the priesthood belongs to Aaron and his sons as "a statute forever."[7]

The Torah describes the Aaronic priestly garments,[8] the use of the laver for washing hands and feet,[9] the tending to the menorah,[10] and other priestly functions as statutes "forever to be observed throughout their generations." Likewise, the commandments for the rituals of the Day of Atonement, including the sacrificial services, are called "a statute forever."[11] The Torah also calls the prohibition on offering a sacrifice except in the Temple with an Aaronic priest "a statute forever for them throughout their generations."[12] Leviticus 23 identifies the appointed times with their prescribed sacrifices as statutes to be observed forever. Numbers 19 declares the ritual of sacrifice of the red heifer and the sprinkling of its ashes as a "perpetual statute"[13] and "a statute forever for them."[14] According to Numbers 18:23, "the Levites shall do the service of the tent of meeting ... It shall be a perpetual statute throughout your generations." If the death and resurrection of our Master has cancelled all of these statutes, then the Torah itself is also cancelled.

Cancelled After All?

A cursory reading of the book of Hebrews seems to confirm that the Torah is cancelled. A New Covenant replaces the Old Covenant:

> For if that first covenant had been faultless, there would have been no occasion to look for a second. (Hebrews 8:7)

> In speaking of a new covenant, he makes the first one obsolete. And what is becoming obsolete and growing old is ready to vanish away. (Hebrews 8:13)

> Therefore [Messiah] is the mediator of a new covenant, so that those who are called may receive the promised eternal inheritance, since a death has occurred that redeems them from the transgressions committed under the first covenant. (Hebrews 9:15)

The evidence from the book of Hebrews appears completely straightforward: The gospel renders the Aaronic priesthood, the sacrificial services, the Temple, and the Torah itself obsolete.

To put it in the vernacular of the Talmud, "This is a difficulty."

Difficulty Two: The Apostolic Community and the Temple

A second difficulty arises when we consider the evidence of the apostolic community. If the gospel did cancel the Torah and the Levitical worship system, the apostolic community in Jerusalem seems to have been ignorant about the change. They continued to revere the Temple and participate in its services throughout the book of the Acts of the Apostles.

Yeshua and the Temple

The disciples of Yeshua revered the Temple because their Master revered it. He regarded the Temple as his "Father's house."[15] As a boy, Yeshua was reluctant to leave the Temple courts. As an adult, he could be found in the Temple teaching and attending the festival services. He spent the last days of his life, prior to his crucifixion, in the Temple. He prophesied its coming destruction only with sorrow and weeping. He drove the moneychangers from its courts, and he quoted the prophet Isaiah, declaring, "It is written, 'My house shall be called a house of prayer.'"[16] He was zealous for the Temple; "His disciples remembered that it was written, 'Zeal for your house will consume me.'"[17] He promised to return to the Temple when Jerusalem welcomes him with the words, "Blessed is he who comes in the name of the Lord!"[18]

The Apostles and the Temple

After the ascension, his disciples "were continually in the temple blessing God."[19] They were most likely in the Temple when the Holy Spirit was poured out upon them on the day of Pentecost. After that, they were "day by day, attending the temple together."[20] The Temple became the locus of the apostolic community. They attended the daily times of sacrifice in the Temple and participated in the prayer services.[21] They congregated and taught in Solomon's portico, the courtyard of the Temple closest to the Mount of Olives, that they might be the first to greet Messiah when he returned.[22] Every day, the believers "were all together in Solomon's Portico" and "the people held them in high esteem."[23] Even when the Sanhedrin ordered them not to speak in the Temple, they persisted. An angel of the LORD instructed them, "Go and stand in the temple and speak to the people all the words of this Life."[24] They remained in the Temple, "and every day, in the temple,"[25] they continued to assemble in the name of Yeshua. As a result, "a great many of the priests became obedient to the faith."[26]

Stephen and the Temple

When false witnesses had Stephen arrested, they charged him with speaking against the Temple in the name of Yeshua. In his disputations, Stephen may have referred to Yeshua's prophecies about the coming destruction of the Temple. However, the book of Acts states unequivocally that the charges about Stephen speaking against the Temple and the Torah were false allegations raised by false witnesses.[27] The high priest asked Stephen, "Are these things so?"[28] He was asking, "Are you and your sect speaking against Moses, against the Torah, and against the Temple?" Stephen denied the charges.

Stephen responded with a brief survey of Israelite history in which he presented a pro-Temple, pro-Torah apologetic. In essence, he affirmed his orthodoxy within normative Judaism, citing the biblical origin for the authority of Moses and the legitimacy of the Temple. But he also went on to make a case for Yeshua, declaring him to be the prophet "like unto" Moses who, like Moses himself, was rejected by the people. He drew in the Temple theme as he pointed out that Israel's historical compromises with paganism defiled the Temple's sanctity in the past. In the same way, their rejection of the Messiah would compromise the Temple in the future.

The Temple Sect

One might even consider the Jerusalem community of believers to be a Temple sect. They did not build a church or even a synagogue; they were all about being in the Temple. Even the name of the sect, the Ekklesia, may be originally derived from the Temple. *Ekklesia* ("assembly," ἐκκλησία) is the Greek word that you see translated as "church" in your Bibles, but in the Hebrew Scriptures, its equivalent, *kahal*, קהל, typically refers to an assembly in the Temple.

It may have evolved quite naturally. If the early Jerusalem believers were, every day, greeting one another, saying, "I'll see you at the assembly," meaning, "I'll see you in the Temple," one can imagine a natural evolution in which the believers actually began to refer to themselves as "the Assembly," and in Greek "the Assembly" is "the Ekklesia."

The believers in Jerusalem practiced a type of communal living, selling their possessions and holding everything in common as they lived in Jerusalem. Why didn't Paul's congregations follow that model? Why was everyone in the Jerusalem congregation selling all they had and moving in together? Because the Temple was in Jerusalem. Simon Peter did not want to go back and live in Capernaum. James and John, the sons of Zebedee, did not want to go back to live in Bethsaida. James, the brother of Yeshua, did not want to go back and live in Nazareth. Nathaniel did not want to go back to Cana. And the Greek-speaking Jews from Diaspora wanted to remain in Jerusalem too, near the Temple, near the apostles, near to the Father's House. So Joseph Barnabus sold his property in Cyprus and moved to Jerusalem. Stephen moved to Jerusalem. Ananias and Sapphira sold their property and moved to Jerusalem.

The Temple drew the apostolic community together. The believers were a Temple sect.

Apostolic Sacrifices

Not only did the believers congregate in the Temple and participate in the prayer services at the times of sacrifice; they continued to bring sacrifices. This should go without saying. If they did not continue to participate in the sacrifices, as the theologically-unclouded reader would assume, the Bible should have recorded that deviation from normative Jewish practice. It does not. Instead, it notes that they continued to participate in the normal sacrificial services.

Nearly thirty years after the death and resurrection of the Messiah, Paul "went up to worship in Jerusalem,"[29] to keep the festival of

Pentecost, and "to present offerings."[30] He joined four other believers who, like himself, had undergone Nazarite vows. The five of them needed to offer a series of animal sacrifices to complete their vows.[31] Paul agreed to pay for the expenses of the other Nazarites, meaning he personally financed the sacrifice of ten lambs and five rams.[32] The narrative of the book of Acts relates the story of these sacrifices matter-of-factly, as if believers offering sacrifices in the Temple was nothing unusual. Instead, James and the elders of the apostolic community pointed to Paul's offering of sacrifices as evidence to other Jewish believers that he was still living "in observance of the law"[33] and therefore "kosher," despite what he might be teaching Gentiles.

Paul defended himself before Festus, saying that he only "went up to worship in Jerusalem."[34] In a Jewish context, to "worship in Jerusalem" means to offer sacrifice and prayer at the Temple, as prescribed by God in Torah. Paul went on to say: "Now after several years I came to bring alms to my nation and to present offerings" (Acts 24:17). The Greek word translated as "offerings" (*prosphora*, προσφορά) means "sacrifice." Paul declared that he went to Jerusalem to present sacrifices.

Was not Jesus the final sacrifice? Had not Jesus already cancelled the sacrifices through his sufficient death? Apparently no one had told Paul this; he was bringing sacrifices. No one told James, the brother of Yeshua, either. If anyone should have known better, it would have been the Master's own brother, but he was the one who suggested to Paul, "Look, people are saying you are not Torah observant. I know you are, you know you are. Prove to them that those are lies. Offer the Nazarite purification sacrifices, not only for yourself, but also for these four other Nazarites."

> [James] used to enter the Sanctuary alone, and was often found on his knees beseeching forgiveness for the people, so that his knees grew hard like a camel's from him continually bending them in worship of God and beseeching forgiveness for the people. Because of his unsurpassable righteousness he was called The Righteous One, and Oblias, "Bulwark of the people and Righteousness." (Eusebius, *Ecclesiastic History*)

If the death and resurrection of the Messiah had cancelled the Levitical worship system, why did the apostolic community still engage in that worship system? Why did Paul bring sacrifices? Why did the apostles continue to assemble in the Temple?

So far, we have seen that the theology that says Messiah's death and resurrection replaces the Temple worship system, the sacrifices, the priesthood, and so forth, creates two enormous theological difficulties:

1. It requires the abrogation of the Torah. We cannot have our theological cake and eat it too. Either the death and resurrection of Yeshua cancelled the Torah or it did not, and if the Temple and the sacrifices and the Aaronic priesthood and the Levitical system were all cancelled, then the Torah was cancelled.

2. The theology that Messiah's death and resurrection replace the Temple worship system does not find support in Apostolic-Era practice. Instead, we find that the early Jewish believers were essentially a Temple sect, still participating in the Temple system after the death and resurrection of Yeshua.

A third difficulty arises in the words of the prophets.

Difficulty Three: The Messianic-Era Temple

According to the prophets (and there is no ambiguity about this matter) the holy Temple will be rebuilt and its services reinstated in the Messianic Era—this is a central expectation. Numerous prophetic texts could be cited. For our purposes, a few critical texts will suffice. Isaiah predicts that in the Messianic Era, "the mountain of the house of the LORD shall be established," and the nations of the world will say, "Come, let us go up to the mountain of the LORD, to the house of the God of Jacob" (Isaiah 2:2–3). The terms "mountain of the house of the LORD," "mountain of the LORD," and "house of the God of Jacob," all refer to the Temple.[35] Likewise, Zechariah predicts that the LORD will return to Zion and dwell in

Jerusalem, "and the mountain of the LORD of hosts [will be called] the holy mountain" (Zechariah 8:3). The prophet Ezekiel promises that, in the Messianic Era, the LORD will send king Messiah and establish his temple forever: "I will set my sanctuary in their midst forevermore. My dwelling place shall be with them, and I will be their God, and they shall be my people." (Ezekiel 37:26–27). Other prophecies of Ezekiel go much further. Beginning in Ezekiel 40, the prophet foresees the Messianic-Era Temple in all its detail, along with a re-established Aaronic priesthood carrying out the sacrificial services. In all, Ezekiel dedicates eight chapters to a vivid description of the future Temple and its services—a future Temple in which the sacrifices are offered, in which the priesthood, the sons of Aaron the priests serve along with the Levites, and they offer sin offerings, peace offerings, burnt offerings, and festival sacrifices—animal sacrifices. This is the prophetic expectation: When Messiah comes, animal sacrifices will be offered again.

Some dispensational schools of Christianity attempt to reconcile these prophecies with the belief that, in the end times, "the Jews" will rebuild the Temple and begin to sacrifice again. Their animal sacrifices, coming after the death and resurrection of the Messiah, will be an abomination to God. They teach that this is the abomination of desolation, and the Temple of the Antichrist. That is wrong and horribly mistaken. Instead, the rebuilding of the Temple and reinstitution of the sacrificial system is part of the expectation of the Messianic Age, God's "Holy House."

Aaronic Priesthood in the Messianic Era

The prophets are unanimous; the Messianic Age requires a rebuilt Temple in Jerusalem. Moreover, the Aaronic priesthood and the Levitical system must re-emerge in the Messianic Era. Jeremiah (the prophet who most clearly predicted the new covenant) made a new-covenant promise about the coming of the Davidic Messiah. In the same oracle, he predicted that, just as the LORD will not break his covenant with David, neither will he break his covenant with the Aaronic priesthood. Jeremiah 33:15–18 pairs the future coming of the Messiah with a restoration of the Levitical priesthood and the sacrificial system:

In those days and at that time I will cause a righteous Branch to spring up for David, and he shall execute justice and righteousness in the land. In those days Judah will be saved and Jerusalem will dwell securely. And this is the name by which it will be called: "The LORD is our righteousness." For thus says the LORD: "David shall never lack a man to sit on the throne of the house of Israel, and the Levitical priests shall never lack a man in my presence to offer burnt offerings, to burn grain offerings, <u>and to make sacrifices forever</u>."

These are new-covenant promises. Yet in seeming contradiction, the epistle to the Hebrews teaches that the new covenant displaces both the old covenant and the Levitical priesthood.[36]

If the death and resurrection of Yeshua abrogated the Temple, the sacrifices and the priesthood, then why would God reinstate those things when the Messianic era begins?

This is a difficulty.

The three difficulties outlined above in this chapter all arise from one basic assumption: The death and resurrection of the Messiah have cancelled the Levitical system. This assumption is based almost completely upon a few chapters from the Epistle to the Hebrews. In the next chapters, we will take a new look at the book of Hebrews to see if we can better understand and reconcile these three difficulties.

Summary

The destruction of the Temple did not cancel the sacrifices forever. The sacrifices are an integral part of the Torah, and Jesus said he did not come to cancel it. The Torah calls the laws establishing the priesthood, the Temple, and the sacrifices "eternal statutes." The book of Hebrews, by calling these "obsolete," creates a difficulty. Yeshua and the apostles revered the Temple. The early believers were a Temple sect, and even Paul, toward the end of his life, brought animal sacrifices to the Temple. Also, many prophets foretold the restoration of the Temple and its continuing significance in the Messianic Era.

Questions

1. What are some difficulties with the idea that Yeshua's death abolished the sacrifices?

2. If Yeshua did not come to abolish the Torah, what does this imply about the sacrifices?

3. In the Torah, the laws regarding the priesthood, the Temple, and the sacrifices are "eternal statutes." What is the implication of this?

4. What difficulty is raised by the book of Hebrews when it calls the first covenant obsolete?

5. What was the actual behavior of Yeshua, of the apostles, and of the early Messianic believers toward the Temple and the sacrifices?

6. What did the prophets say about the future of the Temple, the priesthood, and the sacrifices?

5
Two Different Priesthoods

Christian theology assumes that the death and resurrection of the Messiah cancelled the Levitical system. The priesthood of Messiah replaces the Aaronic priesthood. His suffering and death replaces the Temple sacrifices. The true heavenly sanctuary above replaces the earthly Temple.

These assumptions are based, almost completely, upon a few chapters from the middle of the Epistle to the Hebrews. In this chapter, we will begin to take a look at what the writer of the book of Hebrews really had to say about the Levitical system and the Aaronic priesthood.

Before we begin to seriously study the theology of the book of Hebrews, we need to distinguish between the Temple above and the Temple below, and between this present world and the world to come. The writer of the book of Hebrews assumes that his readers are conversant with both concepts.

The Heavenly Temple

According to tradition, when Moses went up Mount Sinai and disappeared into the thick, dark cloud, he actually entered into the heavenly realms. His ascent into the cloud that covered Sinai brought him into the heavenly court of God's throne. There he saw the angels, and there he saw the throne on which God himself sat. On Mount Sinai, Moses entered the eternal dwelling place of God; he stood in the courts of heaven.

As Moses beheld the splendor of that place of glory, the LORD spoke to him, "Let them make me a sanctuary, that I may dwell in

...eir midst. Exactly as I show you concerning the pattern of the tabernacle, and of all its furniture, so you shall make it" (Exodus 25:8–9).

According to Jewish tradition, the "pattern" Moses saw on the mountain came from the eternal dwelling place of God—his heavenly Temple. The rabbis teach that the Tabernacle on earth was a reflection of the LORD's heavenly Tabernacle. Every detail of its plan reflected an aspect of the LORD's dwelling place above:

> This is what God said to Moses, "Just as you have seen it here above, copy the pattern below … If you will make below a replica of that which is above, I will leave my heavenly assembly and cause my Dwelling Presence to dwell among you." (*Exodus Rabbah* 35:6, quoting Exodus 25:40)

> The Holy One, Blessed be He, desired to have a dwelling place below, just as He has one above. (*Tanchuma Bechukotai* 65)

As God described each article of the Temple to Moses, he showed Moses the real one in his heavenly abode. Every furnishing of the Temple, even the Temple itself, was the earthly counterpart or replicate of a heavenly one, the one Moses saw in heaven. God wanted his holy dwelling place on Earth made according to the pattern of his dwelling place above.

The writer of the book of Hebrews knew the same tradition. He regarded the Temple on earth as an earthly reflection of the "real" Temple in Heaven:

> They serve as a copy and shadow of the heavenly things. For when Moses was about to erect the tent, he was instructed by God, saying, "See that you make everything according to the pattern that was shown you on the mountain." (Hebrews 8:5)

The Temple below reflects the Temple above, but they are two different venues altogether. One belongs to this world; the other belongs to that world above, which is also called "the world to come."

The World to Come

Jewish eschatology divides time into two distinct categories: this present world and the world to come.

1. This Present World (*olam hazeh* [עולם הזה])

2. The World to Come (*olam haba* [עולם הבא])

Jewish eschatology uses the term "this present world" to indicate the created order, the world as we know it, the whole universe, from the beginning of time until its conclusion. This present world will endure until the Messianic Age. In some opinions, it will continue through the Messianic Age; in others, it will conclude at the beginning of the Messianic Age. In either case, this present world will eventually give way to the world to come, a new order, a new heavens and a new earth.

In apostolic theology, the Messianic Age belongs to this present world. The world to come will begin only at the conclusion of the thousand-year Messianic Age: "a new heaven and a new earth, for the first heaven and the first earth had passed away" (Revelation 21:1). Then "the heavens will be set on fire and dissolved, and the heavenly bodies will melt as they burn! But according to his promise we are waiting for new heavens and a new earth in which righteousness dwells" (2 Peter 3:12–13).

An Ongoing Priesthood

In the previous chapter, we observed that the Messiah's cancellation of the priesthood, the Temple, and the sacrifices raises three difficulties. The three difficulties suggest that the premise itself may be faulty. How do we know that the priesthood, the Temple, and the sacrifices were all abolished by the death and resurrection of Messiah?

Beginning with the priesthood, Exodus 29:9 explicitly states that the priesthood belongs to Aaron and his sons in perpetuity: "The priesthood shall be theirs by a statute forever." The words "a statute forever (*chukat olam*, חקת עולם)" describe a commandment that will never be revoked—at least not in the present world, the *olam hazeh.* It is the clearest possible way for the Torah to say, "This commandment will be in force as long as the world endures."

Therefore, the priesthood belongs to the house of Aaron from generation to generation. Even to this modern day, the descendants of Aaron generally know who they are. The stringent *halachah* around priestly families has kept the genealogical lines more or less certain. According to *halachah*, priests may not marry proselytes. Other prohibitions on the priesthood (such as funerals) have combined to preserve family identity from generation to generation. The priesthood yet belongs to the descendants of Aaron, and it always will.

A Change in the Priesthood

Has the *chukat olam* promising the priesthood to Aaron and his family forever been revoked?

The book of Hebrews speaks of a change of the priesthood:

> For when there is a change in the priesthood, there is necessarily a change in the law as well. For the one of whom these things are spoken belonged to another tribe, from which no one has ever served at the altar. (Hebrews 7:12–13)

This passage seems to revoke the Aaronic priesthood and topple the Torah, all in one swift stroke. The priesthood has changed, and along with that came a necessary "change of the Torah as well." This raises a serious conflict. The Bible says that God's Torah is perfect, eternal, and unchanging. The eternal, unchanging Torah says that the priesthood will belong to Aaron and his sons as an eternal statute.

If it were possible for the Torah to change and the priesthood to be revoked, the writer of the book of Hebrews could simply have said, "The sons of Aaron are no longer priests. Messiah is the only true priest now." He did not and could not, because he recognized that such a position would be illegitimate and heretical. How can the Torah be changed? How can the promise to Aaron's house be revoked?

Weak and Useless

The answer to the conflict lies in the carefully structured argument of the book of Hebrews. The writer of Hebrews never claims that Messiah replaces the Aaronic priesthood. He realizes full well that Yeshua was not and is not a priest in the Aaronic order, and he validates the ongoing role of the Aaronic priesthood. He points out that the Master came from the tribe of Judah, not Levi, and that he has no right to the Aaronic priesthood. In fact, he points out that, on earth, he is not a priest at all, since the Aaronic priesthood occupies the office of earthly priests according to the Torah:

> For it is evident that our Lord was descended from Judah, and in connection with that tribe Moses said nothing about priests. (Hebrews 7:14)

> Now if he were on earth, he would not be a priest at all, since there are priests who offer gifts according to the law. (Hebrews 8:4)

Thus, according to the writer of the book of Hebrews, the Aaronic priesthood is legitimate, and its claim to the priesthood is not overridden by Messiah. If Messiah were on Earth (which he was), he would not be a priest because he is descended from Judah, not from Aaron. The priesthood belongs to the sons of Aaron. It is theirs by an eternal statute.

The writer of Hebrews refers to the eternal statute of Exodus 29:9 when he says, "On the one hand, a former commandment is set aside because of its weakness and uselessness (for the law made nothing perfect); but on the other hand, a better hope is introduced, through which we draw near to God" (Hebrews 7:18–19). Note well that the Aaronic priesthood, in this discussion, was not cancelled. The Aaronic priesthood has been "set aside" by a better hope by which a person can "draw near to God."

It sounds as if the writer of Hebrews is saying the Torah is weak and useless. On the contrary, he describes the Aaronic priesthood as "weak and useless." They are weak and useless inasmuch as their ministry does not offer eternal atonement or a passage to the world to come; that is not their job. It is like saying, "As far as changing light bulbs goes, a hammer is useless." Does that mean that hammers are all useless in every situation?

> For the law appoints men in their weakness as high priests, but the word of the oath, which came later than the law, appoints a Son who has been made perfect forever. (Hebrews 7:28)

The Aaronic priesthood is weak and useless when it comes to the task of ushering men into the world to come, because the Aaronic priests are merely mortal men themselves. An Aaronic priest must offer sacrifice first for "his own sins and then for those of the people" (Hebrews 7:27).

On the one hand, the Aaronic priesthood is irrevocable, but on the other hand, it is also unable to bring perfection. In that regard it is weak and useless. Bringing "perfection" is not what the priesthood was designed to accomplish.

Order of Melchizedek

The writer of the book of Hebrews wants his readers to understand that the priesthood in which Yeshua serves is not the Aaronic priesthood at all. Indeed, by virtue of being a son of David, he is automatically disqualified for that priesthood. Instead he serves as a priest in the mysterious order of Melchizedek:

> He has become a priest, not on the basis of a legal requirement concerning bodily descent, but by the power of an indestructible life. For it is witnessed of him [in Psalm 110], "You are a priest forever, after the order of Melchizedek." (Hebrews 7:16–17)

If it were possible for Yeshua to simply kick over the eternal statute of Exodus 29:9 and declare himself the new Aaronic priesthood, the entire Melchizedek argument presented in the book of Hebrews becomes completely superfluous. The writer of Hebrews was not trying to dislodge the Aaronic priesthood; he was trying to demonstrate that the risen Messiah has entered an entirely different kind of priesthood.

He does not serve in the Temple in Jerusalem. The risen Messiah did not offer his blood on the altar in the earthly Temple, nor does he intercede on our behalf before the Father in the holy of holies on earth. He officiates in the Temple above.

According to Jewish theology, the ministering angels serve as priests in the Temple above.

The Temple below reflects the Temple above; the Aaronic priesthood reflects the angelic priesthood above. The writer of the book of Hebrews, however, objects that the high priesthood over that Temple above has not been given to angels: "Now it was not to angels that God subjected the world to come, of which we are speaking" (Hebrews 2:5). This explains the argument in the first two chapters of the Epistle to the Hebrews concerning Messiah's superiority over angels. If anyone has reason to complain that their priesthood has been rendered obsolete by Yeshua, it is the angels, not the sons of Aaron.

The writer of Hebrews also goes to great lengths to demonstrate that Messiah entered not into the earthly sanctuary to minister, but he has become "a minister in the holy places, in the true tent that the Lord set up, not man" (Hebrews 8:2). That is to say, Messiah serves as a priest in a completely different venue than the Aaronic priesthood. The Aaronic priests "serve [in] a copy and shadow of the heavenly things" (Hebrews 8:5), which is to say that they serve in the Jerusalem Temple.

No Contradiction

The Temple of Messiah does not replace the Temple on earth. The Temple on earth only reflected the true Temple, which has always stood and yet still stands.

The Messiah serves in the eternal Temple above. He has taken over the high priesthood of that sanctuary. Therefore, we need not speak of Messiah's priesthood replacing the Aaronic priesthood on earth. Our Master's holy sacrifice and eternal priesthood applies to a completely different venue. His high priesthood is as far removed and above the priesthood of Aaron as the Temple in which he serves is removed and above the Temple in Jerusalem.[37]

In regard to the priesthood, then, the Torah actually has not been changed.

Messiah's priesthood arbitrates over the new covenant, and we look to the intercession of his priesthood for salvation. This offers no contradiction to Torah or the work of the Aaronic priesthood.

Time of the Reformation

The writer of the book of Hebrews states that the Aaronic priesthood "is becoming obsolete and growing old is ready to vanish away" (Hebrews 8:13) along with the rest of this transient, fading, present world. That is because the Aaronic priesthood pertains to this present world, this material, physical state. The Aaronic priesthood offers rituals that "deal only with food and drink and various washings, regulations for the body imposed *until the time of reformation*" (Hebrews 9:10). What is "the time of the reformation"? The "time of the reformation" can only be the transition from this present world to the world to come at the end of the Messianic Era. In other words, the "time of the reformation" is the world to come.

Time of the Reformation = World to Come		
Then I saw a new heaven and a new earth, for the first heaven and the first earth had passed away. (Revelation 21:1)	[It is] the world to come, of which we are speaking. (Hebrews 2:5)	Behold, I am making all things new. (Revelation 21:5)

The Torah is not "becoming obsolete and growing old, ready to disappear"; rather the entire present world along with its needful things will become obsolete when the Temple above descends to Earth as New Jerusalem in the world to come. In the New Jerusalem of the world to come, there is no Temple: "And I saw no temple in the city, for its temple is the Lord God the Almighty and the Lamb" (Revelation 21:22).

The priesthood of Messiah does not invalidate the priesthood of Aaron; neither does the Temple above invalidate the Temple in

Jerusalem. Instead, the Aaronic priesthood is an earthly shadow of Messiah's priesthood, just as the Jerusalem Temple is an earthly reflection of the heavenly Temple. As the writer of the book of Hebrews states at the outset of his epistle, it is "the world to come, of which we are speaking" (Hebrews 2:5).

Regarding the sacrifices of the heavenly sanctuary, the Torah contains no regulations. In that sense, the writer of Hebrews can speak of "a change in the Torah"—not a change in regard to the earthly priesthood, but the introduction of a heavenly one from outside the Aaronic order.

> For when there is a change in the priesthood, there is necessarily a change in the law as well. For the one of whom these things are spoken belonged to another tribe, from which no one has ever served at the altar. (Hebrews 7:12–13)

At the end of this present world, however, things will change. Our Master told us as much when he said, "For truly, I say to you, until heaven and earth pass away [i.e., this present world], not an iota, not a dot, will pass from the [Torah] until all is accomplished" (Matthew 5:18). But when we enter the world to come at the end of the Messianic Age, everything will be accomplished; heaven and earth will pass away, and what is becoming obsolete and growing old will vanish.

That transition does not happen until the world to come. So if the Temple was rebuilt today, only the Aaronic priesthood could serve in it as priests, just as was the case in the days of the apostles. Messiah's priesthood has not cancelled their priesthood. Instead his priesthood is in a different venue, a venue outside of this present world:

> Now the point in what we are saying is this: we have such a high priest, one who is seated at the right hand of the throne of the Majesty in heaven, a minister in the holy places, in the true tent that the Lord set up, not man. (Hebrews 8:1–2)

Summary

Christians assume that Messiah's priesthood replaces the Aaronic priesthood. The book of Hebrews, like the rabbinic midrash, speaks of the earthly Temple as a copy of the heavenly Temple; these correlate with this present world and with the world to come. When Hebrews 7:12–13 speaks of a change in the priesthood and therefore of the law, this cannot refer to the abrogation of the Torah. The difficulty is resolved thus: The Aaronic priesthood only serves for this world, while Messiah's priesthood serves for the world to come.

Questions

1. What is the relation of the heavenly Temple to the earthly Temple?
2. How may the Messianic Age belong both to this world and to the world to come?
3. Discuss: Messiah does not replace the Aaronic priesthood.
4. What are some differences between Messiah's priesthood and the Aaronic priesthood?
5. What is "the time of the reformation" mentioned in Hebrews 9:10?

6
The Heavenly Temple

I n the previous chapter, we discovered that the Melchizedekian priesthood of the Messiah does not replace or compete with the Aaronic priesthood. Messiah's priesthood pertains to the heavenly Temple above and purifies the soul for eternal life. Aaron's priesthood pertains to the earthly Temple below and offers rituals and regulations regarding the physical body.

In this chapter, we will work through Hebrews 8.

Two Covenants

The writer of the book of Hebrews states that the Messiah has become a high priest in the order of Melchizedek. He is seated at the right hand of the throne of Majesty, where he ministers in the true, heavenly Temple. If he were on earth, he would not be a priest at all, "since there are priests who offer gifts according to the [Torah]" already on earth (Hebrews 8:4). The Temple in which the Aaronic priesthood serves is "a copy and shadow of the heavenly things" that Moses saw on Mount Sinai (8:5); it is based upon the pattern God revealed there to Moses. The priesthood of the Messiah is "much more excellent than" the old Aaronic priesthood, just as "the covenant he mediates is better" than the old covenant. Indeed, the new covenant of Messiah's priesthood is "enacted on better promises" (8:6).

The writer of the book of Hebrews speaks of a first covenant and of a new covenant. The first covenant is the covenant between the LORD and his people Israel at Mount Sinai. It consisted primarily of Israel's agreement to keep the Torah. The children of Israel said,

"All that the LORD has spoken we will do, and we will be obedient" (Exodus 24:7).

The second covenant is the covenant of the Messianic Era, described in Jeremiah 31.

The writer of the book of Hebrews compares them, contrasts them, and uses them to establish his argument for the priesthood of Messiah. Christian theology typically understands his language about the first covenant and the new covenant to imply that Messiah did away with the Torah and began a new covenant in its place. Not so. Rather the new covenant to which the writer of Hebrews refers is the covenant spoken of in Jeremiah 31, which states, "Behold, the days are coming, declares the LORD, when I will make a new covenant with the house of Israel ... I will put my [Torah] within them, and I will write it on their hearts." Messiah has initiated a new covenant, but not in antithesis to Torah; instead, the new covenant incorporates the Torah.

The "better promises" of the new covenant include the promises in Jeremiah 31.

The Better Promises of the New Covenant in Jeremiah 31:

1. God will forgive Israel's wickedness. (31:34)

2. God will not remember Israel's sins. (31:34)

3. All Israel will know the Lord. (31:34)

4. Israel will never cease to be a nation before God. (31:36)

5. God will never reject the seed of Israel. (31:37)

6. God will rebuild Jerusalem as an eternal structure. (31:38–40)

7. The entire city of Jerusalem will be Holy to the Lord. (31:40)

Protos and Deuteros

The writer of the book of Hebrews declares that a second covenant was needed because the first covenant was flawed; "for if that first covenant had been faultless, there would have been no occasion to look for a second" (Hebrews 8:7). The word "covenant" does not actually appear in the Greek of Hebrews 8:7; instead, it is supplied by the English translator. The writer is contrasting the covenant made at Sinai with the new covenant. He refers to the covenant made at Sinai as the "first," and the new covenant as the "second."

The problem with inserting the word "covenant" where it was not written is that the writer of Hebrews speaks sometimes in the broad terms of old and new covenant, but at other times he speaks in the narrower terms of tabernacle and priesthood. At still other times, he uses the terms "first" and "second" to contrast "this present world" and the "the world to come."

Two simple Greek words unlock the meaning of Hebrews 8–9. In Hebrews 8:7, the word "first" translates the Greek word *protos* (πρῶτος). The word "second" translates the Greek word *deuteros* (δεύτερος).

> *Protos* = First
>
> *Deuteros* = Second

These words are easy to remember because they are both borrowed in English. The English word "prototype" for example employs the Greek word *protos* to indicate a "first." The Septuagint name for the fifth book of the Torah uses the word *deuteros* and is familiar to us as Deuteronomy, which literally means "Second Law."

We can now read the passage, removing the word "covenant" (which is not in the original), and substituting "first" and "second" for our Greek terminology:

> For if that *protos* ~~covenant~~ had been faultless, there would have been no occasion to look for a *deuteros*. For he finds fault with them when he says [in Jeremiah 31:31]: "Behold, the days are coming, declares the Lord, when I will establish a new covenant with the house of Israel and with the house of Judah." (Hebrews 8:7–8)

The Problem with the Protos

What was wrong with the first? Was it the Torah that was faulty, or was it the people that broke the Torah who were faulty? The problem with the first (*protos*) was that God found fault with his people: "They did not continue in my covenant" (Hebrews 8:9). The weakness of the first (*protos*) resulted from a weak covenant partner, fallen and imperfect human beings. God kept his end of the deal, but we did not keep ours. So what should God do? Should he lower the bar, remove the Torah, and change his standards to accommodate us? God does not change; his Law cannot change. He cannot change his Torah, but he can change us. We are the creatures; he is the Creator. He cannot be recreated, but we can. And that re-creation results in a complete and total redemption, even eternal life, and these are the better promises of the *deuteros*. The *protos* covenant resulted in condemnation for breaking the Torah. The *deuteros* results in re-creation, where the same Torah is written on human hearts.

> In speaking of a new ~~covenant~~, he makes the (*protos*) obsolete. And what is becoming obsolete and growing old is ready to vanish away. (Hebrews 8:13)

Hebrews 8:13 could easily be used as a proof text by which Christian theologians declare, "You see, the Torah is obsolete, aging, and disappearing! Therefore we are no longer under Torah; a believer need no longer observe the Torah or the Sabbaths, festivals, dietary laws, distinctions of clean and unclean, etc. Everything is now permissible. We are under grace, not law, etc."

But the writer of Hebrews did not say "The Torah is obsolete, aging, and disappearing." He said the "first (*protos*)" is becoming obsolete. It is not obsolete yet. It is ready to vanish, but it has not vanished yet.

The Old Covenant Is Not the Torah

Since our writer refrains from using the term "covenant" as he contrasts *protos* and *deuteros*, our translators feel obliged to insert it. After all, the text is certainly using the term "first (*protos*)" in antithesis to the new covenant. One might argue that the old covenant of Torah, as represented by the Aaronic priesthood, has been supplanted by the new covenant of grace, represented by the Messianic priesthood. This comes closer to the meaning, but still is incorrect, because it equates Torah and old covenant.

The old covenant is not the Torah; instead, the old covenant was Israel's agreement to keep the Torah. As a means of salvation it fails, because all have sinned and fallen short. The new covenant is not the collection of Greek scriptures popularly called the New Testament. Instead, the new covenant is an expression taken from Jeremiah 31, a passage quoted at length in Hebrews 8. The new covenant is the covenant for the Messianic Era and the world to come, whereby the Spirit writes the Torah upon the hearts of men, and God forgives and atones for the sin of his people.

Old Covenant = Covenant for this present world

New Covenant = Covenant for [the Messianic Era and] the world to come

The Torah was the new-covenant document of the first-century believers. They did not have a New Testament; they had the Torah, the Prophets, and the Writings. That collection of Hebrew Scriptures contained their copy of the new covenant.

The difference between the two covenants is that, in the new, we are transformed, renewed, recreated, made new creatures in Messiah.

What Is Obsolete?

To be clear, the Torah is not obsolete, aging, and disappearing. The Torah is part of the new covenant. Neither is the Jerusalem Temple obsolete, aging, and disappearing. One can hardly refer to God's holy House as obsolete. It stood forty years after Messiah's resurrection. According to Ezekiel, Isaiah, Micah, and all the prophets, it will be restored in the future. It is hard to call it obsolete, especially when notables like Peter, Paul, James, and John remained involved in its worship services on a continual basis, and it will be rebuilt in the Messianic Era.

Is it the Aaronic priesthood, then, which is obsolete, aging, and soon to disappear? The Torah says it is an eternal priesthood. The prophet Ezekiel speaks of the Aaronic priesthood functioning again in the Messianic Age. Jeremiah links the restored priesthood with the promise of the Messiah.

So what then is it that is the aging, obsolete, and disappearing thing? It is the first, the *protos*—this present world. This becomes clear when the writer of the book of Hebrews explains that the *protos* "is a symbol for the present time" (Hebrews 9:9). What will soon disappear are our human failings. Soon to disappear is the need for one man to tell his neighbor, "Know the LORD." This world, fallen and imperfect as we know it, will disappear, being swallowed up first, in part, during the Messianic Age, and then in the world to come, which will appear at the end of the Messianic Era. The *protos* will be completely subsumed in the *deuteros*. In the world to come, there will be no need for Temple, priesthood, or sacrifice; as it says, "I saw no temple in the city, for its temple is the Lord God Almighty and the Lamb" (Revelation 21:22).

Until then, this present world, the covenant made at Sinai, and the Levitical worship system continues. Although this present world "is becoming obsolete and growing old [and] is ready to vanish away," it has not vanished yet. "Until heaven and earth pass away, not an iota, not a dot, will pass from the Law until all is accomplished" (Matthew 5:18).

Summary

Messiah is high priest "in the order of Melchizedek." He mediates the promises of the new covenant (Jeremiah 31). The key to understanding Hebrews 8–9 lies in the Greek words *protos* ("first") and *deuteros* ("second"). The problem with the first covenant was not with the Torah but with God's people, who did not keep the covenant. The second covenant promises a new heart and mind for the Messianic Era and the world to come. *Protos* refers to this present world; it is passing away, and the *deuteros* is the world to come at the end of the Messianic Era.

Questions

1.   List the promises of the new covenant in Jeremiah 31?
2.   What do the Greek words *protos* and *deuteros* mean?
3.   What was the problem with the first covenant?
4.   Discuss: The old covenant is not the Torah; instead, the old covenant was Israel's agreement to keep the Torah.
5.   Discuss: What is aging, obsolete, and disappearing is the *protos*—this present world.

7

The Symbolic Meaning
of the Tabernacle

In the previous chapter, we worked through Hebrews 8. We discovered that the writer contrasts the first covenant—Israel's agreement at Mount Sinai to keep the Torah—against the second (new) covenant. The new covenant, a covenant for the Messianic Era and the world to come, includes God's promise to write the Torah upon his people's hearts and to forgive their iniquities. The writer of the epistle referred to the Sinai covenant as the *protos* (first) and the new covenant as the *deuteros* (second). In this chapter, we will work through Hebrews 9.

According to the conventional reading of Hebrews 9, the Temple symbolizes the old covenant. As long as it stood and the priests offered sacrifices, the Holy Spirit was showing that Messiah's sacrifice had not been disclosed as the real source of atonement: "By this the Holy Spirit indicates that the way into the holy places is not yet opened" (Hebrews 9:8). A more careful reading of Hebrews 9 reveals a more complex and nuanced symbolism at work.

Most English translations of the Hebrews 9 are unnecessarily cluttered with translators' insertions and clarifications. For purposes of this discussion, I am offering my own rendering of the material. The reader is encouraged to compare the translation with other English versions or to consult the Greek text.

Sanctuary of the Protos

> Now truly the *protos* had regulations for worship and an
> earthly sanctuary. (Hebrews 9:1)

The writer uses the word *protos* instead of the term "old covenant." Ultimately, he will use the word *protos* to communicate a
concept larger than just the covenant made at Sinai. He will explain
that the *protos* symbolizes "this present time" (Hebrews 9:9). The
protos represents the present, fallen, material world which the writer
previously described as obsolete and quickly vanishing. He explains
that the *protos* has regulations of worship, i.e., the priesthood and
sacrificial system prescribed in the Torah. The priesthood and sacrificial system are not the *protos,* but they are functions of the *protos*
inasmuch as they are earthly institutions (of this present world),
simple reflections of the mystical, spiritual, heavenly realities that
will be revealed in the world to come.

The Protos Sanctuary

> For a tabernacle was prepared, the *protos*, in which were
> the lampstand and the table and the bread of the pres-
> ence. This is called the holy [place]. And after the second
> (*deuteros*) veil a tabernacle. This is called the holy of
> holies. (Hebrews 9:2–3)

The instructions for the Tabernacle (and Temple) divided the
sanctuary into two separate domains: the holy place and the holy
of holies. A veil separated the two areas. The holy place contained
the menorah, the table of the bread of the presence, and the altar of
incense. The priests had access to the holy place every day, entering
the holy place twice daily to tend the menorah and offer up incense.
On Sabbaths, they changed out the twelve loaves of the bread of
the presence. They did not have access to the holy of holies behind
the veil where the ark of the covenant sat. The Torah allowed only
the high priest to enter the holy of holies, and that only on the Day
of Atonement.

The writer of the book of Hebrews identifies the holy place as
the *protos* and the holy of holies as the *deuteros.*

Protos **(First)**: Holy Place, containing menorah, table, incense altar

Deuteros **(Second)**: Holy of holies, behind veil, containing ark of the covenant

In the writer's explanation, the holy place of the outer sanctuary corresponds to the *protos* (i.e., this present world and the Sinai covenant); the holy of holies corresponds to the *deuteros* (i.e., the world to come and the new covenant).

Already, this presents a different interpretation than that commonly advanced by Christian expositors, which is that the whole of the Temple represents the old covenant (which they equate with Torah). Accordingly, since the Messiah rendered the Torah obsolete, he also rendered the Temple system obsolete.

Contrary to this conventional interpretation of the symbolism, the writer of the book of Hebrews maintains that the Tabernacle/Temple represents both the *protos* and the *deuteros*. It symbolizes both this world and the world to come, both the old covenant and the new covenant.

Holy place (*Protos*)**:** Sinai covenant, this present world

Holy of holies (*Deuteros*)**:** New covenant, world to come

Inside the Deuteros

Having a golden censer, and the ark of the covenant overlaid on all sides with gold, in which was the gold jar containing the manna, and the staff of Aaron that budded, and the tablets of the covenant, and overtop it cherubim of the glory, overshadowing the mercy-seat. (Concerning [all these things] we are not now able to speak in detail.) (Hebrews 9:4–5)

The holy of holies corresponds to the *deuteros,* i.e., the new covenant and the world to come. In that symbolism, the incense censer, the ark, the golden jar of manna, the staff of Aaron, the two tablets of the covenant, and the mercy seat overshadowed by cherubim are all components that belong to the domain of the new covenant. Each item carries important symbolic value.

The writer of the Epistle to the Hebrews laments that he cannot take the time to expound upon each of these components and their significance within the *deuteros*. Clearly he sees them as central components of the *deuteros*.

- **Gold Censer of Incense:** The golden censer should not be confused with the golden altar which stood on the other side of the veil. This high priest carried this small incense censer into the holy of holies every year on the Day of Atonement. On it he ignited the atoning incense which allowed him access to the presence of God. Its presence in the holy of holies (*deuteros*) implies that the atoning service before God's throne is part of the new covenant.

- **Ark of the Covenant:** The ark of the covenant functioned as the throne of God and therefore corresponds to his holy eternal throne in Heaven. The writer of Hebrews makes a point that, though it is made of acacia wood, it was overlaid on all sides with gold. He sees a symbolic value to this fact, but does not elaborate. Its presence in the holy of holies (*deuteros*) implies that the throne of God is a component of the new covenant.

- **The Golden Jar of Manna:** The manna sometimes represents the prophetic word of God (Deuteronomy 8:3). Yeshua compared himself to manna (John 6), and from "the hidden manna" the Master will feed those who overcome (Revelation 2:17). The manna in the holy of holies (*deuteros*) implies that the hidden manna of eternal life and even Yeshua himself are components of the new covenant.

- **The Staff that Budded:** Ironically, Aaron's staff symbolized the eternal statute of the Aaronic priesthood. The presence of the staff in the part of the Tabernacle called *deuteros* indicates that, in some manner, the Aaronic priesthood continues into the new covenant. In addition, the budded staff represents resurrection. The staff's presence in the holy of holies (*deuteros*) implies that the Aaronic priesthood and the sign of the resurrection are part of the new covenant.

- **The Tablets of the Ten Commandments:** The tablets represent the whole of the Torah, tokens of the covenant. Their presence in the holy of holies (*deuteros*) implies that the Torah is part of the new covenant.

- **Cherubim of Glory:** The cherubim represent the angels about the throne of God. Furthermore, two cherubim bar the way to the tree of life in Eden. Their presence in the holy of holies (*deuteros*) implies that the way to the eternal life and the throne of God is part of the New Covenant.

Holy Place *Protos*	Holy of Holies *Deuteros*
Menorah, Table, Altar	Ark, Manna, Rod, Torah
First Covenant	New Covenant
This Present World	World to Come

Worship in the Protos

> And these things having been thus furnished, the priests always go into the *protos* tabernacle, performing the service. (Hebrews 9:6)

Priests enter into the holy place (*protos*) every day to perform the sacred duties of the Temple service. The *protos* area represents this present world where God can be served. The *protos* corresponds to the mundane reality of our world. This present world is not without godliness. The *protos* is the realm of the divine service. The menorah, the table of the bread of the presence, and the incense altar all stood in the *protos*. The menorah represents divine illumination. The twelve loaves of the bread of the presence represents the nation of Israel. The incense altar represents prayer. The *protos* is the place of worship and divine service.

Once we pass into the *deuteros* of the world to come, our service will no longer be meritorious. The rabbis say, "More beautiful is one hour of repentance and good deeds in this world than all the life of the world to come" (m.*Avot* 4:17).

The Protos Still Stands

> And into the *deuteros*, the high priest alone [enters] one time a year, not without blood which he offers for himself and for the errors of the people. [By this] the Holy Spirit indicates that the way [into] the [holy of] holies has not yet has been manifested, the *protos* tabernacle yet holds standing, which is a symbol for the present time. (Hebrews 9:7–9)

Most translations change the verb tenses to imply that the writer of the book of Hebrews had the destruction of the Temple in view. By changing the verbs to a past tense form, Hebrews 9:8 reads, "The Holy Spirit was showing by this that the way into the Most Holy Place had not yet been disclosed as long as the first tabernacle was still standing" (Hebrews 9:8). This implies that the destruction of the Temple proves that God abolished the old covenant along with the sacrificial system. This interpretation engages in anachronism. The writer of Hebrews was not speaking prophetically here; the Temple still stood as he wrote the letter to the Hebrews, and it will stand again during the Messianic Era.

In order to make these passages fit that theological bias, most English translations change the tense of the verbs to the past tense and add several qualifiers. They are eager to prove the irrelevance of the Temple system and to point out its destruction as proof, but Hebrews was written before the destruction of the Temple.

The ESV renders it more accurately: "By this the Holy Spirit indicates that the way into the holy places is not yet opened as long as the first section is still standing" (Hebrews 9:8). Why is the way into the *deuteros* not yet opened? Because the *protos,* i.e., this present world, still remains. He explicitly says that the *protos* of the Temple, i.e., the holy place, represents this present world.

In rabbinic terminology, this present time is the *Olam HaZeh*, this present world. As long as we remain in this present world, a period of time which extends to the end of the Messianic Era, the Temple still "holds standing." We are still in the *protos*, despite the fact that Yeshua has died and risen. So this passage is not discussing whether or not the Temple is physically standing, because even when it is not, the Temple Mount remains, Jerusalem remains, and the Temple will be rebuilt, because the present world remains.

This is not as confusing as it may seem at first. The *protos* of the sanctuary can be symbolically understood as this present world. Therefore the *deuteros* of the sanctuary (i.e., holy of holies) symbolizes the world to come. Likewise, the writer has made it clear that the *protos* symbolizes the Sinai covenant, whereas the *deuteros* symbolizes the new covenant. He associates the Sinai covenant with this present world and the new covenant with the world to come.

Though we live and serve in the *protos* of this present world, those who have Messiah have already claimed a share in *deuteros* of the new covenant and the world to come. How so? Just as the high priest leaves the *protos* area of the sanctuary once a year to enter into the *deuteros* area of the sanctuary, our high priest has already left the present world (*protos*) and entered the world to come (*deuteros*) by means of his resurrection. The rest of us have not yet gone through that passage. The way is not yet opened for everyone.

Until the Reformation

> The *protos* tabernacle yet holds standing (which is a symbol for the present time) in which both gifts and sacrifices are offered, which are not able, in regard to conscience, to perfect the one who serving, only in foods, and drinks, and various immersions, and physical ordinances, applying until the time of reformation [i.e., the world to come]. (Hebrews 9:8–10)

The writer of the book of Hebrews maintains that the sacrificial services of the Temple apply only to the flesh, not to the spiritual being. The rituals of the Levitical system consist of physical ordinances and regulations which pertain to the physical body. They offer physical cleansing and atonement, but they do not perfect the "conscience" of the one serving, which is to say, they do not perfect the spiritual being—the eternal soul—of the person participating in the rituals. Nevertheless, these rituals apply until the time of the reformation. By "time of the reformation," he means until the world to come.

Let's recapitulate what we have learned. The idea that the Tabernacle/Temple symbolized the old covenant is incorrect. Instead, the Temple is composed of both the *protos* and a *deuteros*, symbolizing both the *protos* covenant (the agreement for this present world) and the *deuteros* covenant (the agreement for the world to come.) The *protos* covenant (the Sinai covenant) pertains only to this physical world, and it remains applicable until the time of the reformation. The *deuteros* covenant pertains to the world to come.

The gifts and sacrifices which are sacrificed at the Temple in Jerusalem only function in regard to the physical things of this world. They "sanctify for the cleansing of the flesh" (Hebrews 9:13). That is correct. The Torah never says, "Bring me a lamb for a sacrifice and your sins will be forgiven and you will have eternal life."

Furthermore, while the Temple still stood, those sacrifices went on every day, twice a day, and the priests ministered twice a day in the *protos* part of the Tabernacle. But the service the high priest alone carried out in the *deuteros* (i.e., the holy of holies) of the Temple occurred only once in the year. Just as the high priest only went into the *deuteros* once a year, so too, the sacrifice of the *deuteros* covenant was a one-time affair.

On the Day of Atonement, the actual sacrifice of the sin offering took place in the *protos* area, corresponding to this present world and under the first covenant. The high priest then carried the blood into the *deuteros* (holy of holies), corresponding to the world to come and the new covenant. Likewise, our Master Yeshua suffered and died in this present world, but his sacrifice is efficacious in the world to come.

As regards life in this present world here on earth, sacrifices belong in the Temple, because those sacrifices pertain to bodily, fleshly, physical existence. They are rituals for the tangible and revealed world on this side of the veil. Those things all apply until the time of the world to come. We enter the world to come after the resurrection.

Therefore, the sacrificial services still apply and will apply until the world to come—the time of the restoration. Those sacrificial services are only efficacious in regard to issues of this present world, and they were never effective to bring someone into the new covenant and the world to come. If the Temple still stood today, the sacrificial and Levitical laws would still apply, but they would not be efficacious for salvation any more than they were before Messiah came.

This helps explain why the prophets indicate that there will be sacrifices in the Messianic Era. The Messianic Era straddles both *protos* and *deuteros*. The Messianic Era might be likened to the veil between the holy place and the holy of holies. It sits upon the threshold of the world to come, but it remains within this present world.

During the thousand years of the Messianic Era, people who have not yet entered the resurrected state will populate the earth. They have not yet entered the world-to-come state of existence, and as such they remain within the *protos* as regards their physical state. The sacrificial service will still be a matter of food and drink and various immersions, regulations for the body applying until the time of the restoration—their entrance into the world to come.

Those physical ritual sacrifices cannot remove sin. They do not change a person's spiritual state on the inside. They "cannot make the worshipper perfect in conscience" (Hebrews 9:9). The *deuteros* covenant, the new covenant, is about changing people on the inside, making them perfect for participation in the world to come—the resurrected state. The *protos* covenant cannot do that. The *protos* sacrificial service cannot accomplish your salvation or your re-creation. Only the *deuteros* covenant—the *deuteros* sacrifice of Messiah—can accomplish that.

Messiah the High Priest

> And the Messiah has come as a high priest of the good things that are yet to come. He entered once into the holy [of holies] through the greater and more perfect tabernacle (not made with hands, that is, not of this creation),

neither through blood of goats and calves, but through
his own blood, securing an eternal redemption. (Hebrews
9:11–12)

The Messiah has come, not as a high priest of the Aaronic order
or even this present world. His priesthood pertains to the *deuteros*,
not the *protos*. He represents the "good things that are yet to come,"
i.e., the world to come and the new covenant. Some English translations deliberately alter Hebrews 9:11 to say, "Christ came as high
priest of the good things that are already here" in order to infer that
the time of the reformation has already occurred and the Levitical
system has already been rendered obsolete. The Greek text, however,
literally speaks of the good things that are yet to come.

When Yeshua of Nazareth rose from the dead, he entered into
the undying realm of the world to come. Like the high priest who
entered the holy of holies (*deuteros*) on behalf of the nation, Yeshua
rose as a first fruits of the resurrection—the good things that are
yet to come. He has already entered the *deuteros* state of existence.

Messiah our high priest entered into the *deuteros*, the holy of
holies, but not the literal holy of holies in the Temple on earth.
Instead, the writer of the book of Hebrews makes it clear that he
carried out his priestly mission in the heavenly Temple. He did not
use the blood of goats and calves, because those sacrifices pertain
to the *protos*, i.e., the earthly Temple in this present world. His sacrifice pertains to the heavenly Temple, where he offered his own life
as the sacrificial payment. By offering his own life, he secured an
eternal redemption in the *deuteros* world to come, something that
bulls and goats could never accomplish.

Messiah's death and resurrection did not cancel the Aaronic
priesthood; instead, his priesthood occurs in a different venue. He
did not cancel the Temple; instead, the Temple on earth reflects the
Temple above.

What about the Sacrifices?

But what about the sacrifices? What do we mean when we say that
Messiah has fulfilled the sacrifices, or that he is the sacrifice for
sin? He was not a Levitical sacrifice. He was not a kosher animal.
He was not slaughtered in a kosher manner. He was not sacrificed

inside the Temple. His blood was not applied to the altar. In no way, shape, or form, was he literally a Temple sacrifice. Not in this present world. Not according to Torah law.

He is a different kind of sacrifice. So when we speak of him as the sin offering, or the peace offering, or the guilt offering, or our Passover lamb, we are speaking only metaphorically. The Messiah was not literally a lamb or a goat. He was not a sacrifice in the Temple.

Christian teaching about the role of sacrifices generally maintains that in Old Testament times, a person could have his sins forgiven by bringing a sacrifice. He transferred his guilt for sin to some unhappy goat. The goat took his punishment for the sin. That's how people were saved. But after Jesus came, we no longer have to bring goats.

This is not such a great way to look at it. Was the death of God's beloved Son merely a matter of convenience for us? If so, Yeshua died to save goats, not men. The writer of the book of Hebrews claims, "For it is impossible for the blood of bulls and goats to take away sins" (Hebrews 10:4).

If this is so, why did people offer sacrifices? As explained in earlier chapters, people brought sacrifices "to draw near" to the manifest presence of God in his dwelling place on earth. They brought sacrifices as gifts, so to speak, to God. The ritual, ceremonial effects of the sacrificial service pertained to this world, particularly to the dwelling place of God in this world, within the Temple precincts. They functioned on a physical, flesh level for the purification of the flesh. Our Hebrews passage states this explicitly.

Blood of Bulls and Goats

> For if the blood of bulls and goats, and ashes of a heifer, sprinkling those defiled, sanctifies to purify the flesh, how much more so shall the blood of the Messiah (who through the eternal Spirit offered himself unblemished to God) purify your conscience from dead works to serve the living God? (Hebrews 9:13–14)

The writer of the book of Hebrews employs a *kal vachomer* (קל וחומר) argument, i.e., *a minori ad maius*: "If such and such is true, how much more so is such and such true." For this rhetorical device to work, the first thing must be true for the second thing also to be true. So the writer of the book of Hebrews says, "If the sacrifices sanctified and purified the flesh in regard to this present world and within the earthly Temple, how much more so does the blood of Messiah sanctify and purify the spirit in regard to the world to come and the heavenly Temple."

Just as the Temple sacrifices purify the flesh, Messiah's sacrifices purify the divine soul ("conscience") from dead works, that is, from sins.

In other words, he assumes it is self-evident that the sacrifices have a role and function in this world, but their scope is limited. Like the purview of the Aaronic priesthood, the scope of the Levitical sacrifices and rituals is limited to this world and to the venue of the earthly Temple. Messiah's sacrifice and priesthood, on the other hand, applies to the venue of the heavenly and the eternal. The Messiah's death did not cancel the Temple sacrifices; rather his death represents a sacrifice in a completely different venue and carries out a completely different function. It is impossible for the blood of bulls and goats to take away sins and to purify a person for participation in the world to come; that was not their function. The Temple sacrifices are relevant for worship of God in this present world. Messiah's sacrifice can purify a person from sins, and it is relevant for entrance into the world to come.

Mediator of a New Covenant

> And because of this, he is mediator of a new covenant. [Messiah's] death came for redemption from the transgressions committed under the *protos* covenant, so that those called may receive the promise of the eternal inheritance. (Hebrews 9:15)

The Messiah is the high priest of the new covenant of the *deuteros*. He offered his life to redeem those who had sinned in the *protos*. Through his priestly ministry, he is able to bring people into the eternal inheritance of the resurrection and the world to come.

The Tabernacle/Temple design depicts both covenants, the *protos* and the *deuteros*, and both covenants actually work together, just like the two parts of the Temple. Both are important. They work together because one pertains to the current physical mortal state—life in this present world—and one pertains to the immortal world to come.

The Temple, the Aaronic priesthood, and the sacrificial system were never about attaining eternal life or the world to come. If we can grasp that, then we will understand why it is unnecessary to suppose that the gospel supplanted them. It also explains why the early apostolic community remained connected with the Temple and with its rituals and services. They understood Messiah's sacrifice for the world to come, not for this world. It also explains how there can be a future, Messianic-Age Temple, because the Messianic Age, glorious and perfect as it will be, will still be a part of this world, not the world to come. After the Messianic Age, a new heaven and a new earth replace the old. New Jerusalem will descend, and then there will be no Temple of sacrifice.

Summary

The book of Hebrews identifies the holy place in the Temple as the *protos* and the holy of holies as the *deuteros*. The holy place corresponds to this present world and the Sinai covenant; the holy of holies corresponds to the new covenant and the world to come. The items in the holy of holy represent realities of the new covenant. Hebrews 9:7–9 should properly be read in the present tense, because the Temple was still standing when Hebrews was written. The Temple rituals endure until "the time of restoration" (i.e., the world to come). The Torah sacrifices do not remove sin; they cannot "make the worshipper perfect in conscience"; still Messiah's death did not cancel the Aaronic prieshood. Rather, it is effective at a different level and prepares us for the world to come. There will be no Temple or sacrifice in the New Jerusalem.

Questions

1. In the Temple, what did the *protos* and the *deuteros* represent (Hebrews 9:2–3)?

2. Discuss: The holy place represents Sinai, this present world, while the holy of holies represents the new covenant, the world to come.

3. Name the items in the Ark of the Covenant and explain their symbolism (Hebrews 9:4–5).

4. How are the verb tenses important for understanding Hebrews 9:7–9?

5. Discuss: The writer of the book of Hebrews maintains that the sacrificial services of the Temple apply only to the flesh, not to the spiritual being.

6. Discuss: The Messianic Era straddles both *protos* and *deuteros.*

7. What were the Temple sacrifices unable to accomplish?

8
The Lamb that Was Slain

When anti-missionaries challenge our faith in the Good News of Yeshua, they follow a common line of attack: They like to poke holes in the Christian premise that Yeshua died as a sacrifice for sins. They are also quick to claim that, in Judaism, no one can suffer for another person's sins.

Previous chapters discussed the premise of Christian theology that the death and resurrection of Yeshua of Nazareth, fulfills, cancels, and replaces the Levitical, sacrificial system. A corollary of that original premise requires that Yeshua's death be understood as a sacrifice for sin. As the Lamb of God, he became a sin offering, sacrificed for the sins of Israel and of the whole world. This fundamental Christian supposition lends itself to the idea that Jesus' death cancelled the sacrificial system by rendering it redundant.

The logic is simple: Previously, God required various types of animal sacrifices as sin offerings. Then he sent his Son as the ultimate sacrifice for sin. After he made the ultimate sin offering, any further sacrifices offered by men would at best be unnecessary and, at worst, an affront to the blood of Messiah and the rejection of his atoning sacrifice.

The previous chapters have already shown that the premise that the death of the Messiah cancelled the sacrifices raises several irresolvable difficulties. Those difficulties led us to re-examine the original premise. We studied the apostolic perspective on the sacrifice of Messiah and his priesthood, and we discovered that, contrary to the prevailing interpretations, the apostles did not teach a fulfillment, cancellation, or replacement of the sacrificial system or Aaronic priesthood. Instead, we learned that the sacrifice of Messiah pertains to the heavenly Temple and the world to come, whereas the sacrifices and the Levitical system pertain to the earthly Temple (which reflects the heavenly) and to this present world.

Yeshua the Sin Offering

This chapter re-examines the concept of Yeshua's role as a sacrifice for sins. The concept can be quickly derived from the Bible, particularly from the writings of the apostles. For example, John the Immerser identified Yeshua as "the Lamb of God who takes away the sin of the world" (John 1:29). The apostle Paul says, "God put [him] forward as a propitiation [atonement] by his blood" (Romans 3:25). The book of Hebrews makes this identification as a sacrifice explicit:

> He has appeared once for all at the end of the ages to put away sin by the sacrifice of himself. And just as it is appointed for man to die once, and after that comes judgment, so Christ, having been offered once to bear the sins of many, will appear a second time, not to deal with sin but to save those who are eagerly waiting for him. (Hebrews 9:26–28)

> When Christ had offered for all time a single sacrifice for sins, he sat down at the right hand of God. (Hebrews 10:12)

According to the Bible, according to the New Testament and the apostles, Yeshua is the sacrifice for sin, the quintessential sin offering. This concept explains the otherwise enigmatic verse, 2 Corinthians 5:21, when Paul says, "he made him to be sin who knew no sin." I think what Paul is saying here is that God made him who knew no sin to be a sin offering. The book of Revelation goes further, depicting Yeshua as the lamb slain. Based upon these apostolic statements, one may feel confident in declaring the death of Yeshua as a sacrifice for sin and the fulfillment of the sacrificial system.

Critics and anti-missionaries, however, raise several obvious objections, all of them based upon God's own laws regulating sacrifices and sacrificial procedure.

A Kosher Animal

First of all, The Torah states that a sacrificial victim must be an unblemished, kosher animal from the herd or flock: a bull, a cow, a goat, a sheep, or ram, or a turtledove. The animal must be unblemished; a fact which we equate with the sinless and unblemished soul of our Master, but even that symbolic equation misses the larger point.

The point is that the sacrifice is supposed to be an animal, not a human being—bulls, sheep, and goats as described in Leviticus 1, Leviticus 11, and Leviticus 22.

Now the believer might think that this is trifling or not playing fair, but on the contrary, this is the literal requirement of the Torah. A sacrifice to God must be a clean animal, and not just any clean animal but a clean animal belonging to a subset of domesticated clean animals. It must be unblemished, it must be kosher, and most importantly, it must be an animal.

A human being does not have split hooves, nor do human beings ruminate, so by the Bible's own law—by God's own rules for sacrifices—human beings do not qualify.

In the Temple

The Torah says that a biblical sacrifice must be carried out in the Temple. Our Master suffered and died outside the walls of Jerusalem; he did not die in the Temple. The writer of the book of Hebrews makes note of this, comparing him to the red heifer, the only sacrifice which God sanctions to be brought outside the city walls (Hebrews 13:12–13, cf. Numbers 19). Aside from the red heifer, though, the Torah requires Israel to offer every sacrifice within the holy Temple, the place that God chose (Leviticus 17, Deuteronomy 12).

Try to see this from a literal perspective. God says that sacrifices must be of the herd or the flock, bulls, cows, sheep, goats. They must be offered in the Temple. Their blood must be applied on the altar. These are God's rules, not man's.

By the Priests

A biblical sacrifice must be facilitated by the Aaronic priesthood, the sons of Aaron. According to the Torah, every sacrifice brought to the LORD must be conducted by the Aaronic priesthood (Leviticus 5–7, 21–22). Our Master's crucifixion happened at the hands of the idolatrous Romans, not God's priesthood, not even Jews. They executed him; they did not sacrifice him.

Kosher Slaughter

A biblical sacrifice must be slaughtered. The Torah prescribes a specific method of slaughter whereby the person sacrificing cuts the throat of the animal being sacrificed, drains its blood into a basin, and applies the blood to the altar. The slaughter itself is supposed to be done with a sharp knife. The slaughterer attempts to spare the animal from suffering and is concerned that the animal should not experience pain or discomfort. In Jewish law, if an animal did suffer from an inappropriate slaughter (perhaps a bad slaughter, a slip of the knife) the sacrifice was declared invalid. Any marring, suffering, sickness, wounds, or other blemish prior to or during the sacrifice also invalidated the sacrifice.

If a priest took a sheep, tore out some of its hair, scourged it with whips, punctured it with nails, and hung it in torment, the sheep would no longer be considered fit for sacrifice—nor would it ever be.

Human Sacrifice

The Holy One, blessed be he, regards human sacrifice as repugnant; the Torah forbids it. God's own laws, his own standards of righteousness, forbid human sacrifice (Leviticus 18, 20). In the book of the prophet Jeremiah, when the prophet upbraids Judah for the heinous sin of human sacrifice, the LORD says, regarding such sacrifices, "I did not command them, nor did it enter into my mind, that they should do this abomination, to cause Judah to sin" (Jeremiah 32:35).

On the other hand, one might object that he did ask Abraham to bring his son as a sacrifice, a burnt offering. The point of that story is that God only tested Abraham, and in fact, he interrupted the sacrifice, and replaced Isaac with a ram, an appropriate animal for sacrifice.

Flawed Logic

All of the above objections deserve to be taken seriously. When looking backwards at the Torah and the Tanach (Old Testament) through the lenses of Christian theology, the believer can easily dismiss such incongruities, but when viewed from the opposite vantage point—that is to say, when viewing Christian theology from a Torah perspective, a Jewish perspective—these incongruities seem insurmountable. Consider the logic.

God gives strict laws defining what is acceptable for sacrifice, how to do it, where to do it, and who is to do it. He intended all of these laws, ostensibly, to foreshadow the ultimate sacrifice. Then, when he finally does get around to offering the ultimate sacrifice, it does not conform to any of the standards that he established, and in fact, completely contradicts them. Suffice to say, these are contradictions deserving a serious answer. Cynics and anti-missionaries point this out in their battles against the gospel, and for the most part we seem to have no answer. It seems as if they baffle the apologists, as if none of this had ever occurred to any believer before.

Literal or Literate

The correct answer, the obvious answer, can only be that Yeshua of Nazareth was certainly not a biblical sin offering. Nor was he a burnt offering, a grain offering, a peace offering, or a guilt offering. He was not a bull, an ox, a heifer, a ram, a lamb, a goat, nor a turtledove. He was not a sacrifice in any of those senses. He was not slaughtered by the priesthood, nor in the Temple, nor was he physically unblemished, nor was his mode of death humane. In no way, shape, nor form, did he literally fulfill or conform to the sacrifices prescribed by the Torah.

But the key word here is literally. We need to learn the difference between a literal reading of the scriptures and a literate reading of the Scriptures. They are not the same.

Yeshua was not literally a sacrifice for sin. Nor was he literally a lamb. Yet John the Immerser prophetically called him the Lamb of God, and Isaiah the prophet prophetically called him a guilt offering. Did John the Immerser literally mean that he was actually a sheep—a sheep in man's clothing. Did Isaiah literally mean that he was a Temple sacrifice? Of course not. They were not speaking literally, nor did they need to speak literally, because the people they ministered among were literate. They understood the concept of metaphor and symbolism, and so do we.

The Sacrifice Metaphor

When the apostles speak of Yeshua as a lamb, a spotless lamb, the Lamb of God, etc., or when they speak of him as a sin offering, a sacrifice, they are speaking metaphorically. They are employing symbolism to say that, "his suffering and death is like unto a Temple sacrifice." How so? Just as the Torah commands us to bring sacrifices to the Temple, God brought his Son to us. Just as the Torah mandates us to spill their blood, the blood of God's son was spilled for us. Just as the priests offered sacrifices in the Temple to atone for sin and uncleanness, and to bridge the gap between man and God, to bring the worshipper near to God, so too, the death and resurrection of Yeshua of Nazareth atones for sin, bridges the gap, and brings us near to God.

In the heavenly sense and in regard to the Temple above, the throne of God, and the world to come, our Master's sacrifice functions quite literally. In that sense, the sacrifices of animals in the Temple on earth are only prophetic shadows and reflections of the sacrifice of Yeshua in the heavenly, just as the Temple on earth reflects the Temple above and the priesthood on earth reflects his priesthood above.

But if we import that spiritual and heavenly reality into the physical reality, thereby confusing type and antitype, we get all mixed up. For example, the writer of the book of Hebrews reminds us that on earth, in this present world, Yeshua is not a priest or member of the Aaronic priesthood: "For it is evident that our Lord was descended from Judah, and in connection with that tribe Moses said nothing about priests" (Hebrews 7:14). Hebrews 8:4 says, "Now if he were on earth, he would not be a priest at all, since there are priests who offer gifts according to the law." Although he sits even now at the right hand of Glory as the high priest in the order of Melchizedek, in regard to this world, he is not a priest on earth. In the same way, he is the sacrifice for sin, once for all, in regard to the heavenly Temple, but on earth, in regard to the Torah and the Temple on earth and "according to the Law," he is not a sacrifice at all.

This demonstrates the difference between a literate and a literal reading of the Bible. One can read so hyper-literally that we destroy the Bible's message. Yeshua is not a sacrifice according to the Torah, not in regard to the Temple; he is not a Levitical sacrifice. He may be considered such only metaphorically, only symbolically, but certainly not literally.

Why Did Jesus Die?

This realization raises an even more profound question. If Yeshua is not a literal sacrifice, then what type of sacrifice is he, and how does this function?

A young Christian once came to me with a similar question. He grew up in an evangelical, Bible-teaching church, went to youth group all through his teen years and attended church and Bible study faithfully. He came to visit a Messianic congregation where I was teaching because he had a pressing question for which he could find no satisfactory answer. He hoped that a Messianic teacher might be able to help. After service, he asked me the one question that had been nagging him. He asked me, "Why did Jesus have to die?"

I did not give him the standard reply, "He died for our sins," because I sensed something more bothering him. He explained, "No one has ever been able to answer this question for me. I understand he died for me, but how does that help me? Why did he have to die? How does his death help others?"

I could have replied, "Well, it's a divine mystery." I could have said, "Somewhere out there, there is a rule that says, if God ever wants to forgive human beings, he has to first pay the price for their sin, and that price is that his only begotten Son has to die." We all understand the theological constructions around it, but seen from the outside, they seem like afterthoughts formulated only after accepting the concept of Messiah's death as an atonement.

Strip it back to a simple, mechanical, cause-and-effect question: How does the death of Yeshua of Nazareth atone for your sins two thousand years later? What gave the apostles the idea that the death of Messiah could atone for someone else's sin?

Why Do the Righteous Suffer?

How does the Master's death accomplish atonement and salvation for the sinner? Of course, there is no answer to this question, and we accept the premise on faith. It is true, not because we can figure it out or because it makes sense to us, but because God has vouched for this truth. He has sealed it and proven it with the resurrection of his Son and the word of his apostles, who proclaimed the message in the power and authority of the Messiah's name.

But setting that truth aside for a moment, let's take a look at the Jewish theology behind the atoning death of Yeshua of Nazareth.

Early Judaism used to believe in a concept we can call the suffering of the righteous. It appears frequently in early rabbinic literature. It formed an important part of the theological landscape behind the Gospels and the other Apostolic Writings.

Judaism is predicated on the concept that God is just and that he administers justice in the world by a strict measure-for-measure, eye-for-eye, tooth-for-tooth, code of justice, the standard of his own law. According to this simple justice system, the righteous are rewarded and the wicked are punished. God rewards those who do good and he punishes those who sin. That simple, black-and-white theodicy is axiomatic in the Torah, in the Prophets, and in the Proverbs.

The problem is that life is not so simple. That theology of measure for measure, rewarding the righteous and punishing the wicked, inevitably leads to a crisis. Jeremiah cries out, "Why does the way of the wicked prosper? Why do all who are treacherous thrive?" (Jeremiah 12:1). The Psalmist says:

> For I was envious of the arrogant when I saw the prosperity of the wicked. For they have no pangs until death; their bodies are fat and sleek. They are not in trouble as

others are; they are not stricken like the rest of mankind. (Psalm 73:3–5)

Behold, these are the wicked; always at ease, they increase in riches. All in vain have I kept my heart clean and washed my hands in innocence. (Psalm 73:12–13)

The entire book of Job presents a long, poetic, philosophical argument about the same question: Why do the wicked prosper? Why do the righteous suffer?

The Doctrine of the Pharisees

In the days of the Master, the Pharisees offered answers to these questions. First of all, they insisted that death is not the end of life. The dead find comeuppance in the afterlife; in paradise the souls of the righteous receive reward, while in Gehenna, the wicked receive punishment. A resurrection of the dead will provide everyone with an opportunity to receive a final judgment for deeds committed in the flesh. The righteous will enter the final reward of the world to come and the wicked will not. That's a thumbnail sketch of the Pharisaic answer: God makes everything balance out in the afterlife. So we read in tractate b.*Kiddushin* 40b, for example, "The Holy One, blessed be He, brings suffering upon the righteous in this world, in order that they may inherit the future world."

Suffering Brings Atonement

But this answer does not sufficiently explain the suffering of the righteous, the pious, and the innocent on earth. In early Jewish theology, the sages gave a second answer: that the suffering of the righteous brings atonement. The concept is probably rooted in passages like Isaiah 53, where the suffering servant of the LORD is depicted making many righteous, bearing iniquity, and making intercession for transgressors.

The concept works like this: The sages assumed that suffering results from sin. If so, for whose sins do the righteous suffer? They do not suffer for their own sins; after all, they are righteous. For whose, then? If not for their own, it must be for the sins of others.

So too, death results from sin. The wages of sin is death. But if so, for what do the righteous die? They must die for the sins of others.

Examples from the Rabbis

Therefore, one often encounters Talmud dictums proclaiming that the suffering of the righteous and the death of the righteous bring atonement. A few examples will suffice to illustrate the point:

> Why is the story of Miryam's death placed next to the laws of the red heifer? This is to teach you that just as the red heifer brought atonement, so does the death of the righteous bring atonement. Why is the story of Aaron's death followed by the story of the transfer of his priestly garments? This is to teach you that just as the priest's garments were meant to bring atonement, so too the death of the righteous brings atonement. (b.*Moed Katan* 28a)

A parallel text from the *Midrash Rabbah* offers an additional example:

> Rabbi Chiyya bar Abba said, "The sons of Aaron died on the first of Nisan. Why is their death mentioned in connection with the Day of Atonement? This is to teach you that just as the Day of Atonement brings atonement, so too the death of the righteous brings atonement. And how do we know that the death of the righteous brings atonement? From the fact that it is written [in 2 Samuel 21:14], "And they buried the bones of Saul and his son Jonathan … and after that God responded to the plea for the land" (*Leviticus Rabbah* 20:12)

These are examples the sages used to illustrate their theological premise that the suffering and death of the righteous brings atonement for others. In the Talmud, Rabbi Eliezer (a sage almost contemporary with the apostles) tells a story in which the LORD tells the Angel of Death, "Take a great man among them, through whose death many sins can be atoned for them" (b.*Berachot* 62b). Many other similar examples could be cited.

Correcting Anti-Missionaries

The rabbinic concept of atonement through the suffering of the righteous contradicts the anti-missionaries who teach that, in Judaism, no person can suffer for another person's sins. Anti-missionaries often state this to obscure the gospel, but rabbinic literature does teach that the suffering and the death of the righteous can atone for the sins of others.

An interesting anecdote from *Exodus Rabbah*, an early rabbinic commentary on the book of Exodus, illustrates the concept. In this story, Moses had just received the designs for the Tabernacle, the priesthood, and the sacrifices. Being a prophet, Moses could see into the future; he realized that one day the Temple would be destroyed and the sacrifices cease.

> Moses said to God: "Will not the time come when Israel shall have neither Tabernacle nor Temple? What will happen with them then?" The Holy One, blessed be He, replied, "I will then take one of their righteous men and retain him as a pledge on their behalf, in order that I may pardon all their sins." (*Exodus Rabbah* 35:4)

Suffering of the Righteous One

Again, the sages believed that the suffering and death of the righteous could bring atonement for sinners. Even so, there is no one wholly righteous. "Surely there is not a righteous man on earth who does good and never sins" (Ecclesiastes 7:20). All have sinned and fallen short of the glory of God—all, that is, except one. Yeshua of Nazareth lived to full adulthood and yet lived a completely sinless life, completely fulfilling the righteousness of the Torah. His sinless life deserved the reward of eternal life. He deserved to never suffer; he deserved to never die, and yet he suffered and died a horrid death, like a criminal. A divine injustice! And moreover, he went to this death willingly. He sacrificed himself, so to speak. Not as a Levitical sacrifice; rather, he freely offered up his life.

Given the theological framework assuming that the suffering of the righteous brings atonement, his Jewish followers naturally interpreted his unmerited suffering and unmerited death as occurring on behalf of others. If the death of the righteous brings atonement, then how much more so must the death of the completely righteous one—the sinless one—bring atonement?

And this is the answer to the young Christian's question. To understand how it is that Yeshua's death, two thousand years ago, atones for your sins today, you must first understand the Pharisaic concept that the suffering of the righteous brings atonement— that the death of the righteous atones for sin. The atoning death of Yeshua, it turns out, is a thoroughly Jewish theological concept.

Worthy Is the Lamb

Yeshua is our *korban* (offering), our "thing brought near," our sacrifice before the eternal God. He is the sacrifice for our sins, but not in the Temple on earth, not a literal sin offering sacrifice whose blood is smeared on the horns of the altar in the earthly Temple.

When the apostles speak of Yeshua as the sacrificial lamb, they are speaking metaphorically. The efficacious nature of his suffering and death does not arise from sacrificial procedures, from the literal application of his blood to an altar, or from his taking the place of the Temple's sacrificial system. Instead, his suffering and death affects atonement based on the principle that, measure-for-measure, eye-for-eye, he did not deserve to suffer or die, because he alone was completely righteous. Therefore, his suffering and death can be credited to others.

Anti-missionaries who object that Yeshua could not be a sacrifice for sin because his death falls outside the boundaries of the Levitical codes need to reconsider their argument. He is not literally a lamb, nor was he literally a Temple sacrifice. His death did not cancel the sacrificial system of the Temple.

The book of Revelation says he is the Lamb slain from the foundation of the world (Revelation 13:8). If his death abrogated the sacrifices, then they should have been unnecessary before his death as well, for his atoning work is eternal, unbounded by time.

Instead, his death stands as far outside the Levitical worship system as his priesthood stands outside of the Aaronic order. No animal sacrifice could ever avail for atonement in the heavenly sanctuary, nor could any man's suffering and death serve the Levitical function performed by an animal sacrifice inside the earthly sanctuary. Though we might speak of the death of Messiah as a sacrifice, we do not mean to imply that his sacrifice applied within the Levitical system. If his sacrifice did not apply within the Levitical system, we should not be concerned about any perceived competition between his sacrifice and the Levitical system. His death need not cancel the sacrifices or render them redundant, and future Messianic-Era sacrifices do not encroach upon the atonement already accomplished by his death.

> Worthy is the Lamb who was slain, to receive power and wealth and wisdom and might and honor and glory and blessing! (Revelation 5:12)

Summary

Anti-missionaries claim that no one can suffer for another person's sin, allowing no room for belief in Yeshua as a sin offering. Certainly Yeshua was not a kosher animal; he was not slain in the Temple by the priests in a kosher manner; and the Torah forbids human sacrifice. Yeshua was not a literal Torah sacrifice, yet the New Testament speaks of him as such, using many metaphors. The sages of Israel believed the suffering of the righteous could bring atonement for sinners. If those who are relatively righteous effect redemption, how much more the suffering and death of Yeshua, who was completely righteous!

Questions

1. Discuss: How was Yeshua's death like the sin offering? How was it different?
2. What are some objections to seeing Yeshua as a literal sin offering?
3. What was the view of Israel's sages about the suffering of the righteous?
4. Discuss Yeshua's death as atonement, apart from the Levitical system.

Conclusion

This booklet gives only a brief overview of the sacrificial system and is an attempt at reconciling the Levitical worship system and the gospel. A more in-depth and exhaustive study would require many more pages. For the current purpose, this overview is sufficient to introduce the issues and offer a plausible solution.

If the death of the Messiah cancelled the sacrifices, then the death of the Messiah cancelled the Torah. We cannot have it both ways. The Levitical worship system cannot be separated from the Torah any more than any of the other laws.

In this booklet, we suggest that the death of the Messiah did not abrogate the Levitical worship system. Instead, the fall of the Temple, a full generation after the Master's death, brought a temporary cessation to the sacrificial service. In the Messianic future, however, the Temple services will resume and continue until the time of the reformation—until the world to come.

As demonstrated in the previous chapters, this interpretation has several advantages. It harmonizes the Bible. It preserves the integrity of the Torah. It does not break God's promises to the house of Aaron. It does not cut short the "eternal statutes" of the Bible. It explains why the apostles remained engaged in the Temple and the sacrificial system even after the resurrection. It explains the prophecies that predict the sacrificial system and Aaronic priesthood at work in the Messianic Age, still to come. It removes the theological tension between Yeshua's atonement and the Levitical system. It shows that Yeshua's sacrifice was not redundant, by demonstrating that animal sacrifices never achieved atonement in the Temple above. It does not place the Master's sacrifice in competition with the Levitical worship system. It explains the Temple allegory and Melchizedek material in the book of Hebrews. It answers antimissionary objections about human sacrifice. It explains how the apostles could consider Yeshua as "a sacrifice" despite the Levitical laws prohibiting human sacrifice.

Summary

The death of Messiah did not abrogate the Levitical worship system; rather it accomplished atonement at a different level—that of the world to come. The supposed conflict is resolved.

Questions

1. Did the death of Messiah abrogate the Levitical system? Give reasons for your answer.

Endnotes

1   Hebrews 6:2.

2   Alfred Edersheim, *The Temple, Its Ministry and Services* (Grand Rapids, MI: Eerdmans Publishing, 1992), 115.

3   Rashi on Leviticus 1:9.

4   Hebrews 9:11, 24; 11:19–20.

5   Hebrews 8:11–12, 26–28; Hebrews 9:11, Hebrews 11:21.

6   Hebrews 9:11–15; 10:1–12.

7   Exodus 29:9, cf. Deuteronomy 18:5.

8   Exodus 28:43.

9   Exodus 30:21.

10 Exodus 27:21, cf. Leviticus 24:3.

11 Leviticus 16:34.

12 Leviticus 17:7.

13 Numbers 19:10.

14 Numbers 19:21.

15 Luke 2:49, John 2:16.

16 Matthew 21:13 quoting Isaiah 56:7.

17 John 2:17.

18 Luke 13:35.

19 Luke 24:53.

20 Acts 2:46.

21 Acts 3:1.

22 Acts 3:11.

23 Acts 5:12–13.

24 Acts 5:20.

25 Acts 5:42.

26 Acts 6:7.

27   Acts 6:13–14.

28   Acts 7:1.

29   Acts 24:11.

30   Acts 24:17.

31   Acts 21:23–26.

32   Numbers 6:13–21.

33   Acts 21:24.

34   Acts 24:11.

35   Cf. Isaiah 25:6–8; 65:25.

36   Hebrews 7:11–12.

37   Hebrews 7:24–28.